To Fr. Mike
& Jeanne

all our love & prayers,
always!
+Pat & Ben

INSIDE

The more a priest realizes the fullness of his gifts, the more he can fulfill his divine mission. Through the eyes of those healed, forgiven, blessed, or freed from the devil's grip, Fr. Clement J. Machado discloses how Christ lives in him. He brings to light the power of the supernatural that priests work with every day, choosing a living catechesis: Witnesses who reveal where the miraculous power of the priesthood is made manifest. This book restores a lost understanding of the invisible realities of the Faith. It clearly shows what it means to be a priest, for the abstract truths priests work with have become so indistinct that people no longer understand the natural or supernatural order, or the nature of evil, or the blessings Holy Hands can bring. Fr. Machado reminds you that in recognizing your priest's noble compassion, you invite Christ in ... and find wonders awaiting you there.

Holy Hands

Fr. Clement Joachim Machado

CMJ Marian Publishers
Chicago

The Scripture quotations contained herein are from the New Revised Standard Version Bible, Catholic Edition, copyright © 1989 by the Division of Christian Education of the National Council of the Churches of Christ in the U.S.A. and are used by permission. All rights reserved.

Some names of those whose stories are recounted in this book have been changed to respect the privacy of these faithful people who have exhibited great courage with their witness.

Published in the United States by:

CMJ Marian Publishers & Distributers
P.O. Box 661
Oak Lawn, IL 60453
708-636-2995
www.cmjbooks.com

ISBN: 978-1-891280-89-9

First Edition
Library of Congress Control Number: 2010936688

Copy editor: Jack Gillespie
Graphics: Pete Massari

Printed in the United States of America

I dedicate this book to all the wonderful priests who do the Lord's work.

And to my father and mother, Joachim John and Annie Paul Machado; my sister Grace Joachim and her husband, Sanjay; my brother Jason Joachim and his wife, Heather; and my brother John Joachim and his wife, Cyndi, and to their children, my nephews and nieces.

"This audacity of God who entrusts himself to human beings —who, conscious of our weaknesses, nonetheless considers men capable of acting and being present in his stead—this audacity of God is the true grandeur concealed in the word 'priesthood.'"

~ Pope Benedict XVI, Homily on the Solemnity of the Sacred Heart of Jesus, St. Peter's Square, June 11, 2010

"The world looks to the priest, because it looks to Jesus! No one can see Christ; but everyone sees the priest, and through him they wish to catch a glimpse of the Lord! Immense is the grandeur of the Lord! Immense is the grandeur and dignity of the priest!"

~ Pope John Paul II, Holy Mass for the students of the Pontifical Major Seminary in Rome, Oct. 13, 1979

THE STORIES
Holy Hands

Foreword

A Fitting Postscript to Pope Benedict XVI's Year for Priests

Over the past 35 to 40 years the priesthood has been going through a great deal of scrutiny from all sectors and priests have in the last ten years come under close examination because of the scandals that have come to light. Even though the number of priests who have offended is small, that number is far too many. One wonders at the depravity involved but also one yearns for a renewal of this holy vocation wherein priests can show forth the marvelous, sacramental connection to Jesus Christ that is their priesthood.

I know countless priests who are unsung heroes in the sacrifices they make for the sake of their people and the genuine desire for holiness that is their daily bread. Often their stories of the myriad ways that Jesus works through them and cares for his flock, soul by soul, person by person, go untold. *Holy Hands* is just such a work, shared by people who have been the recipients of Fr. Clement J. Machado's priestly ministry. While these stories are miraculous in many instances, they are signs of the loving care that the Lord Jesus has for His flock through consecrated hands, anointed by the ordaining Bishop at the time of priestly consecration.

Fr. Machado's ministry is in some ways unique but these testimonies give us proof that when a priest says "yes" to the will of God without reservation and is willing to make the sacrifices involved in that affirmation, beautiful things happen. The Lord uses the priest's hands, his time, his words, and his actions to deliver others from slavery to sin, to illness, and to paralysis of body, mind and spirit.

How many times have you heard that the Anointing of the Sick has assisted someone and goes almost undetected since there are always other extenuating circumstances that seem to provide a plausible explanation? Yet with eyes of faith we know that the healing grace of Jesus Christ reaches through the person of the priest and works a transformation in the person or the circumstance.

These days because people have wandered so far away from the practice of their faith and because so many others are ignorant of the power of the Gospel, the ministry of the priesthood, and the Catholic Church, many are being ensnared by the powers of darkness and evil and become discouraged and hopeless.

It is with great joy that I recommend the careful and meditative reading of these true stories of the workings of the loving Divine Providence through the ministrations of the holy hands of a priest.

His Excellency,
The Most Reverend David Laurin Ricken
Bishop, the Diocese of Green Bay
Bishop Emeritus, Cheyenne, Wyo.
Author, *Be Thou My Vision: Meditations on the Priesthood*

Licentiate Degree (J.C.L.), Pontifical Gregorian
    University, Rome
Former Vocation Director & Vicar for Ministry
    Formation, & Diocesan Chancellor, Pueblo Diocese
Official of the Congregation for the Clergy at the
    Vatican, 1996-1999
U.S. Conference of Catholic Bishops, Bishops'
    Committee on Catechesis; Editorial Oversight Board,
National Directory of Catechesis
Chair, the Committee on the American College of
    Louvain, Belgium
Member, the Committee for Canonical Affairs and the
    Committee for Domestic Justice & Human
    Development, the Bishops' Advisory Council for
    the Institute for   Priestly Formation
Board of Trustees, Our Lady of the New Advent
    Theological Institute, Denver
Board of Regents, Conception Seminary College

"Modern man listens more willingly to witnesses than to teachers, and if he does listen to teachers, it is because they are witnesses."

> ~ **Pope Paul VI,** *in Evangelii Nuntiandi, from Rome, Solemnity of the Immaculate Conception of the Blessed Virgin Mary, Dec. 8, 1975*

Preface

A Kerygma, Heralding God's Power of Miracles in a Skeptical Age

Awaken, my friends! Awaken, brethren priests! You are called to minister, to give witness to Jesus Christ—today. To reach out to the children of God who are unaware of, or indifferent to, the sacred and sacramental in their lives. Get ready to engage in combat for the Church, to live a *kerygma* for the invisible mystery and glory of the Catholic priesthood! *Behold this precious and divine Mystery!*

You can proclaim this faith only through authentic witness. As Pope Paul VI said, the world cries out for teachers. In this book, laymen, laywomen, and priests testify to the supernatural dimension of the royal priesthood, obscured in a skeptical age. These courageous witnesses introduce all to God's power of miracles, through the miracle of the priesthood. This book is for young and old, churched and unchurched. It opens one's eyes to the vista of the magnificent, the unfolding panorama of the continuing ministry of Christ, through His priests.

Kerygma is a Greek word used in the New Testament for preaching *(see Luke 4:18-19, Romans 10:14, Matthew 3:1).* It's related to the Greek verb κηρύσσω (kērússō), to cry or proclaim as a herald.

As Jesus began His public ministry, He entered the synagogue and read from the scroll of Isaiah. He identified Himself in *Luke 4:17-21* as the one Isaiah foretold *(Isaiah 61).* Jesus proclaims the good news to the poor, the captive, the blind, and the oppressed. The Age of Fulfillment dawns! This takes place through Christ's birth, life, ministry, death, and Resurrection. Through His Resurrection, God exalts Jesus at His right hand, as king of the new Israel. The Holy Spirit in His Church is the sign of Christ's ever-present power and glory. The Messianic Age is accomplished with Christ's return. He appeals for repentance. He offers forgiveness and the Holy Spirit. He offers Salvation.

He chooses priests to complete His divine mission for Him. Neither laymen nor priests can afford not to live a *kerygmatic* in these times. *Each of us must teach and proclaim the salvation at hand.*

Behold the mercy of God, my friends. Learn how to make the supernatural natural and how to make it yours. Open your hearts and minds to better understand how to help your priests grow in spiritual perfection, so that together, with your shepherds, Christ can fulfill His divine mission through you.

Fr. Clement Joachim Machado
Oct. 17, 2010
Feast of St. André Bessette [†]

[†] Although not yet officially a saint on this book's debut, Blessed André Bessette would soon be canonized by Pope Benedict VXI.

"You are clothed with His Royal Priesthood, and your own priesthood is but one with His, and you are but one priest with the Sovereign Priest. You are Jesus Christ living and walking on Earth. You represent His Person, you hold His Place."

~ *St. John Eudes*

Biographical Note

I was born in the small town of Mission, British Columbia, Canada. As it turned out, my birthplace predicted my vocation. Raised in Montreal, called *Ville-Marie* or the City of Blessed Virgin Mary by early French settlers, I was ordained a Roman Catholic priest on Nov. 26, 1993, at the city's St. Patrick's Basilica, the "mother Church" of the Irish and the English-speaking of Canada.

Ordaining me at the then-146-year-old church, where images of the most prominent saints in the Church's history encircle the interior, was Archbishop of Montreal Jean-Claude Turcotte, now a cardinal. Assisting were three bishops and 70 concelebrating priests; attending were 1,500 lay people. During the Litany of the Saints, as I lay prostrate on the sanctuary floor, I felt the presence of St. Patrick overcome me. I heard his voice in my heart and soul, clear and articulate: God wanted me to evangelize to all ends of the Earth, including St. Patrick's beloved Ireland. At the time, at age 27, I was humbled and deeply moved that I would be called to the missions. While I believe the message delivered by one of Christianity's most venerated saints to be of supernatural origin, I wondered how it could be possible. After all, I was being ordained as a diocesan priest.

And yet, only seven years into full-time evangelization work from my home base in Rome, I'll have traveled almost a million miles around the world. I traveled nearly 175,000 miles during one recent year alone, pursuing my international evangelization ministry on seven continents. Through the grace of God, I did this through preaching; teaching; television and radio interviews and programs; and by leading retreats, parish missions, conferences, days of recollection, Bible study, and the healing of family lineages.

Through an apostolate of my ministry, Our Lady of Refuge, and with help from doctors and nurses worldwide, I've led medical and spiritual missions to the poor of the Philippines. Over the last three years, we've treated more than 6,000 people, including children, the elderly, and the handicapped. I also conducted pilgrimages and spiritual retreats to the world's holiest sites—the Holy Land, Rome, and Marian Shrines such as Our Lady of Lourdes, Our Lady of Fatima, and Our Lady of Guadalupe.

I've been mentored and trained under the official exorcists of Pope Benedict XVI through the Holy See's Vicariate of Rome, Fr. Gabriele Amorth, S.S.P., and Fr. Giancarlo Gramolazzo, F.D.P. I've been exorcist *ad actum* and *modo stabile* for various dioceses worldwide, including a diocese north of Rome, Arezzo-Cortona-San Sepulcro.

After I was ordained, I became parochial vicar at St. Monica's Parish and then spent three years at St. David's Parish in Montreal. I served as parochial vicar *pro tempe* at

St. Ignatius Parish in Ottawa and then worked as full-time chaplain at the 753-bed Élisabeth Bruyère Hospital run by the Sisters of Charity of Ottawa. In parish work, I saw how people came physically sick to their priests. I prayed for them and with them before the Blessed Sacrament; I blessed them.

A Worldwide Mission

I saw the tremendous effect of grace, people being healed, particularly when I was a hospital chaplain. I saw symptoms from serious and chronic conditions diminish. I noticed, too, that doctors and medical staff discerned the effects of my ministrations, made possible through the Holy Spirit. Often, doctors and medical staff were moved to conversion or near conversion by these events. And they saw that their patients felt better. Even if patients weren't healed outright following prayers and reception of the Holy Sacraments, their symptoms lessened.

When I was a parish priest and hospital chaplain, however, the call to the missions never left me. In fact, I only felt the call more strongly.

I conducted a pilgrimage to Rome in May 1999 for the beatification of Blessed Pio of Pietrelcina. It was there that I learned of the Society of Our Lady of the Most Holy Trinity (S.O.L.T.) S.O.L.T's founder, Fr. James Flanagan, invited me to Robstown, Texas, where I discussed with him my great desire to evangelize by apostolic preaching through the media, parish missions, retreats, and religious teaching. Fr. Flanagan embraced the idea. He invited me to join his Society, and in April 2000, I was incardinated there.

Beginning in Ottawa, I had received calls to preach at missions around the world. Mother Angelica's Eternal Word Television Network in Irondale, Ala., invited me to develop two series, one on Purgatory in 1997 and another on Padre Pio based on my 1999 pilgrimage.

Later, I hosted a series on Christian morality and appeared on an EWTN program to speak about youth and the occult. I began working with EWTN on a biography of Blessed André Bessette, who would be canonized in 2010 and who was instrumental to my own priestly vocation.

As my missionary work grew, I went wherever I was invited—throughout the United States, Canada, India, and Africa. I've been to China, Holland, Egypt, Thailand, Switzerland, Luxemburg, Lichtenstein, Germany, Poland, Israel, and France. Other stops included Portugal, Spain, Belgium, Nigeria, Mexico, and Israel.

In 2001, the S.O.L.T. general council asked me to become vice rector of the order's House of Studies for seminarians in Rome. The formation program includes immersion in the city's rich ecclesial environment. The men reside at the de LaSalle Christian Brothers Generalte and receive academic formation at the Angelicum University (the Pontifical University of St. Thomas Aquinas), where Pope John Paul II, ordained a priest, wrote his doctoral dissertation under the guidance of French Domini can theologian Reginald Garrigou-Lagrange.

I was vice rector at the House of Studies for two years, while also studying ancient biblical languages at the Pontifical Gregorian University; spiritual and dogmatic theology at the Pontifical University of the Holy Cross; bioethics, moral theology, and dogmatic theology at the

Pontifical Athenaeum Regina Apostolorum; and Mariology at the Pontifical Faculty of the Marianum. I also studied at some of the most distinguished pontifical institutions.

I improved my knowledge of languages I'd need to speak in my worldwide missions. Besides those I grew up with and learned in primary and secondary school—English, French, Italian, Latin—I became fluent in ancient and biblical Greek, biblical Hebrew, and Marathi (an Indian language), and increased my fluency in written Spanish and Portuguese.

I didn't begin my missionary work full time until 2003, when I was replaced as S.O.L.T.'s vice rector. Since then, by the grace of God, my healing and deliverance ministry has grown exponentially. I often speak to priests and laity, promoting the healing of the whole person—body, mind, heart, and soul. This is possible through the sacraments, intercessory prayer, and the ministry of Holy Sacramentals.

One sacramental my parents, Anne and Joachim, were devoted to was the family Rosary. We prayed every day as a family—my brother, two sisters, and I. My parents centered all academic, social, and familial activities on Christ, and seeking to know His will, so my family home was a place of great hospitality. And as I was growing up, my parents fostered a love of the priesthood and of missionaries.

Family Piety Forms Priesthood

That's when I met an extraordinary priest from India: the late Monsignor Jacob Chiakmury. He influenced me by instilling in my heart a love for the priesthood and the Lord and personally inviting me to consider becoming a Man of God. I recall his first suggestion in 1970, when I was about four years old. He later would ask me to serve at the altar with him whenever he said Mass.

His invitation to the priesthood was lighthearted, but it planted a seed. I loved his dedication, the way he conducted himself, always seeking people out, speaking to them about the Lord. He offered consoling words and was always ready to bring supernatural perspective to problems, to be ready for Confession. That's the type of priest he was. I would see him with his breviary at all hours of the day. It seemed incredible to me that he would go to new and unknown rectories, living out of a suitcase, raising funds for corporal works of mercy, for seminaries, for infirmaries. And he was a diocesan missionary, traveling throughout the world from India.

My maternal grandmother, Isabel Tuscano, influenced my call to Christ, too, by her pious humility, love, and devotion. In my childhood bedroom there was a beautiful picture of Christ, a holographic 3-D image that showed Christ on the Cross and then, when you moved, you could see Christ walking on water. She loved that picture—two pictures, really, because it would play on the light and your eyes. It was in the center of my room, between the beds of my brother John and me.

I recall waking up late at night, seeing moonlight streaming in the window, with my grandmother bathed in that soft light, prostrate or kneeling, praying before the image. Her lips moved in prayer and adoration. I never wanted to disturb her. She was so beautiful. It moved me.

But it probably was my father who most influenced my vocation. My dad had a great love of the Fathers of the Church. He loved talking about St. Thomas, and as I got older, he and I would discuss the existence of God. He had been in the seminary in the early 1940s in India. But because of his family's poverty he left the seminary to support his family; they were farmers.

Later, through Church aid and individual support from local parish priests who saw his talent and potential, he was able to use his industriousness to put himself through school. He earned a master's degree in education and a certification in special education from McGill University in Montreal and master's level competency in Latin and Sanskrit. In 1964, he married my mother and soon after, they moved to Africa, where he became headmaster of Edo Boys High School (now Adolo College) in Benin City, Nigeria. He and my mother emigrated to Montreal in 1965. Decades later he still greatly influences me.

The move to Montreal was providential to my calling as a priest; it was at St. Joseph's Oratory in Montreal where the seed Msgr. Chiakmury planted took root.

As a teen, I became attracted to the beautiful Oratory atop Mount Royal and the story of Blessed André Bessette, the humble Holy Cross brother who as a porter at the Collège Notre-Dame du Sacré-Coeur, at the foot of Mount Royal, shared his profound faith on behalf of the afflicted. He took up their petitions to St. Joseph, and he asked them to pray to his patron. It moved my heart to see how this poor, humble, courageous man had tremendous compassion for the poor and suffering. Everyone can relate to St. Joseph. He's a universal figure. He appeals to people of every condition, every walk or state of life. His holiness as universal patron of the Church further contributes to his saintly magnetism. And he caused me to reflect on the priesthood and God in a universal way.

In my heart, I saw the priesthood as serving a parish, and beyond. Msgr. Chiakmury influenced me to become a traveling missionary. He lived real dedication and sacrifice. He was priestly, but down-to-earth. He always conducted himself with dignity. He dressed appropriately and his mannerisms were above reproach. During his missionary travels, he learned much about various cultures and about the people in both Third World and Western churches. What moved me most was his great devotion to Jesus and the Blessed Sacrament, whether in the Liturgy of the Hours, at Mass, or in Confession. He always was reverent. I appreciated his attention to detail.

When I visited St. Joseph's Oratory as a teenager, I went seeking greater clarity for what God wanted from me. I was seeking discernment from the Oratory. From my home, it was an hour each way by bus. I would go to Confession there. I received a very strong grace at St. Joseph's Oratory. I would pray in the vigil corridor in the Oratory's basement. The scent of hundreds of votive candles, combined with the sight of the racks upon racks of castoff crutches and canes from pilgrims healed there, created an atmosphere that tremendously contributed to my vocational choice.

At St. Joseph's Oratory, my many graces included the knowledge of my sins as God sees them and real supernatural contrition. This was a deepening of my faith, and St. Joseph led me from my teen years right through to my seminary days. I was 21 when I entered the seminary. I'd been attending the College of St. Augustine—run by the Servites of Mary in Cape-Rouge on the periphery of Quebec City—discerning my vocation. In September 1987 I entered Le Grand Séminaire de Montréal, and graduated five years later, after a year of pastoral internship and field work at St. Monica Parish in Montreal's Notre-Dame-de-Grâce archdiocese.

But it was at St. Joseph's Oratory that I had experienced my most profound reflection: My life wasn't worth living unless I was wholly giving.

For me, life was to be the life of St. Joseph, to serve the Word Incarnate, our Lord Jesus Christ, nurturing Him, protecting Him. I felt that was in my calling, and more and more I thought that would be by way of the priesthood. That's what true joy and happiness was to me then, and now, thanks be to God, *is*.

I realized then that I would never truly be happy or joyful unless I gave my life as St. Joseph and our Lord did. Through the intercession of Our Lord's earthly father, through my parents, through my grandmother, our Blessed Mother, and all those who interceded for me, I was able to hear His word, and through His grace, act upon it. ~ ♠

"See, it is I who have created the smith who blows the fire of coals, and produces a weapon fit for its purpose; I have also created the ravager to destroy" (Isaiah 54:16).

Holy Hands

Chapter 1

Not long ago, while in Rome, I was visited by two seminarians who, with a newly ordained priest, had recently returned from a pilgrimage to Mayo, Ireland. During the prayers and devotions in the central square at Our Lady of Knock, Ireland's National Marian Shrine, they heard loud voices.

It was with great surprise that they realized the voices came from the belly of a tiny woman nearby.

They saw the woman's face contort, and she seemed to almost lift off the ground. The priest prayed quietly a few steps away, immediately realizing that something demonic was disturbing this woman.

It started raining. The priest thought, while in thanksgiving and in realization of his holy orders, *"I'm a priest, I can bless this falling water: Lord, please bless this rain."* As he blessed it, he asked the Lord to drive away the evil spirits and to relieve, comfort, and strengthen the poor woman.

Right away, the voice within the woman began howling: *"Awwwww! Get this water off me! AWWWWW! It's burning me! It's burning me!"*

The priest, wearing a bulky overcoat that hid his white collar, knew what was happening and prayed more fervently. He heard horrible voices, dozens of them: *"There's Holy Hands here!*

"There's Holy Hands here!" the spirits screamed. "This water's burning me!"

I share this true story because, dear friend, it concisely and spectacularly illustrates the priesthood's power, how holy, anointed hands can affect natural elements, such as water falling from the sky. And it shows how supernatural forces—evil spirits infiltrating the soul of a poor woman—can, through the person of Christ on Earth, be stilled and even expelled.

By sharing an experience like this, I can help you better understand supernatural realities and how the natural can affect the supernatural, and vice versa. God's sanctifying grace can bring respite and more, if we, like this priest, become aware of the graces available to us and beg the Lord for mercy.

I could, in an academic presentation, talk about the priesthood and the nature of a calling, and the power God gives to the priest. But through this story about the suffering woman, though incomplete here, I can help you digest years of theology. In fact, through a very real experience like this, any man or woman can grow to understand major theological insights.

More Mindful, More Faithful

It's my sense, and the critical reason for this book, that the priesthood's power and the abstract invisible supernatural realities that a priest works with each day have become so distant and indistinct that people no longer understand the natural or supernatural order, or the nature of evil, or the true blessings his Holy Hands can bring. Our Holy Father, Pope Benedict XVI, recognized this lost reality when he proclaimed a Year for Priests on the 150th anniversary of the death of St. John Mary Vianney, the Curé of Ars, proclaiming him patron saint of all priests.

Healing and liberation increase our faith and our reliance on His mercy. We live in the *Age of Mercy* because where sin abounds, His Mercy abounds all the more. The priest is an apostle of mercy. It is precisely because we live in such a wounded world, a world increasingly alienated from God, that we receive Divine Mercy from Christ through His priests.

When the seminarians in Ireland saw this woman freed of the devil's grip, they witnessed the priesthood's power working in a poignant way, in a way perhaps they'd taken for granted. If they didn't take the priesthood for granted, they at least needed to deepen their knowledge of it, to rediscover it, or be reminded of some past knowledge, because a certain obscurity has enveloped the priesthood in the last generation or two. You probably can agree that things have become very casual in our times. Not that our times have bred so much contempt for the priesthood, although there's plenty of that in certain countries, like France or in parts of India where priests and religious are killed for the Faith. But generally there's more indifference to priests—and the role they play in the Sacred. I hope to lead you to be not as forgetful, but more mindful, of the supernatural.

I also hope to show you how much these hands that are anointed by God can heal and liberate all who suffer from ailments, oppression, or possession. Too often today, and this is where evil has infiltrated men's hearts, we hear of the harm done by these hands and not of their limitless potential for good.

Yet when I share stories of people relieved of years of sickness or decades of crippling possession, I can see how listeners' thoughts and feelings come alive. I can see how they relate to these miracles on many levels—intellectually, morally, emotionally, and even physically. They sense the grace and the peace and the power—not just on a spiritual plane, but on every level of their being.

The stories throughout these pages can make any of us realize that while we can open up avenues for evil and allow it to seep into our souls through sin, other avenues can infuse a soul with light, with happiness, with healing, forgiveness, conversion, and the self-discovery and know-ledge that conviction in the Truth brings.

This neglect by people in recognizing the supernatural order and its connection with our natural lives isn't unique to lay people; it's often misunderstood or overlooked by those schooled in years of theology or doctrine. I, and other priests, see fellow priests with years of serving parishioners realizing, during a healing service, the power that the Holy Spirit has directed through their Holy Hands. What I hope to help you understand through this book is that the natural and supernatural worlds are parallel and that when God intervenes, the supernatural becomes natural.

People of Hope, Through Christ

In these pages, you'll read stories of healing, conversion, exorcism, and other human transformations through the power of God's grace, moving through His chosen instrument, the priest. You'll also read of transformations through sacramentals—the rites, actions, and holy items the Church uses to imitate her Holy Sacraments. People have obtained through saintly intercession certain effects, particularly those of a spiritual nature. Used in accord with the Church, sacramentals help people receive grace, do good, and avoid evil, to protect the body and soul, and to help forgive venial sin.

Sacramentals include prayers, candles, holy water, blessings, vestments, the sign of the Cross, ashes, salt, medals, and the Rosary. What makes sacramentals special is the blessing of a priest, anointed in the sacrament of Holy Orders to Consecrate bread and wine into the Body and Blood of Christ. People are healed through sacramentals combined with the supernatural power of the sacraments, particularly the sacraments of the Holy Eucharist and Holy Confession; Our Lord once told St. Maria Faustina Kowalska that the greatest miracles of all happen in the confessional.

Many faiths have a dark outlook on nature and even human nature. Their pessimistic view of the world means that everything is corrupt, or is at least prone to corruption, including the Church and its hierarchy, according to classical Protestantism. We can't save ourselves, they say. But we can be saved through the Holy Sacraments, by the pure grace of God, and by the individual faith of the believer. I've witnessed this time and again in my ministry.

I'm a Roman Catholic missionary, raised and educated in a Faith that teaches us that our nature is created good by God, is sullied by sin, and can be restored to splendor by grace. Humanity isn't inherently evil or corrupt. Grace transforms. Grace divinizes. As a priest of the Society of Our Lady of the Most Holy Trinity, founded in Corpus Christi, Texas, in 1958 by Fr. James Flanagan, I help serve the world in the areas of deepest apostolic need.

Since I began my missionary work, I've traveled more than 150,000 miles each year—to evangelize, to lead retreats, to celebrate Mass, to hear confessions, and to bring healing and liberation to all those who seek the transforming and sanctifying grace of God. Through God's grace, I act as an exorcist of the Holy Roman Catholic Church, and through that process of grace's liberating power upon a human soul, I've witnessed the beautiful and transformative power of our Lord. My travels have taken me from my home base in Rome to China, Ecuador, the Philippines, Fiji, Portugal, Iran, Dubai, and many other places around the world, including every state but Alaska and Idaho.

Through my travels, I've become keenly aware of the differences in the spiritual and physical needs of those living in advanced and Third World countries. I spend 70 percent of my time re-evangelizing people in the Western world. In American society, I see the forces of secularism combating Christian faith in an increasingly secular age. While the United States was always strong in its religious fervor, I consider it a post-Christian society that's basically neo-pagan. In Eastern Europe, I've witnessed the ravages of communism and the rise of secular hedonism, from two sources —prosperous Western Europe with its indifference to faith, and Eastern Europe, with its forced atheistic communism, an ideology which has eroded faith over decades. But even there, I see more openness to faith than in the prosperous countries of Western Europe and America.

Through the grace of God, my missions are bearing fruit in Asia and Africa, where it's easier to evangelize and provide religious instruction. Far greater are the challenges of the Western hemisphere and Eastern Europe. Even so, in Kazakhstan and Belarus, both former Soviet republics, I've witnessed a renewed hunger for the Faith in certain parts of the population.

In meeting people around the world, I see that when they begin to understand invisible supernatural reality and the sacrament of Holy Orders, and the sacrament and grace in the Eucharist, and the High Priest who is Christ, given supernatural capacity for the service of God, suddenly it combines to forge their new identity of Christ.

Parishioners can be served by their parish priest for years, celebrating Holy Mass and the sacraments, but when they reflect on a story like I've shared earlier, suddenly it hits them: *There are Holy Hands here! My God, the spiritual power you have given our beloved priests!*

A Noble Compassion

It is a power that flows from the greatest form of God's love, charity. The greatest expression of that Divine Love is mercy. It is the fruit of love. Through the priest, it is noble compassion. Through the priest, it is continually new, continually dawning. People don't think about it that way. They don't see the connection. Love is the branch; charity the stem. The flower of love, supremely, is mercy. When someone is merciful to you, compassionate to you, it is the greatest act. God's greatest act is mercy. It's why our Lord went to the Cross to heal us, even though He didn't need to.

I hope in this book to help you realize the Sacred around you. I hope to help you realize the mercy available to you for any kind of disturbance in your life, be it psychological, physical, preternatural, or supernatural. Divine Mercy is for resolution, relief, consolation, and healing of the whole person—body, mind, heart, and soul. Mercy is the greatest attribute of charity, the greatest and primary scope of His redemptive love. God is healing us in mercy, through mercy, for mercy.

When people want to be healed, they're begging for mercy, for forbearance. Remember Bartimaeus in the gospels? He was so blind he could barely understand from which direction the Lord was coming. He hears noise, and he shouts louder than the crowd: "Son of David, have mercy on me!" Notice he doesn't say, "Heal my blindness." When he's asking for mercy, he's asking for something he may not realize, to be healed from physical and spiritual blindness, his whole person.

"Son of David, have mercy on me!" He says it once, twice, three times, and finally, Jesus notices. He turns around. People probably are saying, *Old man, keep quiet in your rags, we have our own needs!*

But when they see our Lord stop and take notice of this suffering man, they recognize Christ's notice, and instantly Bartimaeus becomes someone. They're happy for him. They all wanted our Lord's attention. Isn't that what you and I want? We beg: "Master, that I may see."

Bartimaeus says this not knowing he wanted to be cured more deeply, not only of his blindness of body but also of soul. Already, he was being cured through the power of grace, so that he could see more clearly in the eyes of faith. I write here about that type of healing. How can we be healed like that?

If we think like Bartimaeus, we can better understand that the act of healing is an act of eminent mercy.

People tormented by the devil see an end to that harassment as an act of mercy, and that's why they trust their exorcist, why they travel hundreds of miles to be prayed over. If you seek to be healed, you need that trust. Either you have it, or you don't.

The priest is one of the greatest conduits of this mercy.

People ask priests: Are *you* sacred? If you ask, you don't understand the power of the priesthood. For centuries, priests have blessed fields, orchards, expecting mothers, and homes. After Hurricane Katrina in the United States, I visited homes I'd blessed prior to the storm and found negligible damages. Other homes, even those right next door, were gutted, destroyed. *Behold the mercy of God!*

But we cannot take this power for granted or be presumptuous in the Lord. We need to realize the sense of the Sacred, and recognize it even in a priest's simple gestures—the making of the sign of the Cross, the absolution given in Holy Confession, the imposing of hands on the sick—these all apply mercy, and in ways that can even overcome demonic possession.

We take so much for granted these days and, unfortunately, in some cultures the priest is a clown, a show. *Do you know devils will show more respect out of compulsion than most people on the street will when they see a priest's collar?* We do not understand how every word, every gesture, is a grace.

I was visiting a parish recently and a man came up to me, someone who had been through a long process of healing and purification and was now living a life of devotion and respect for the Eucharist, and he took my right hand. He kissed it, revering the priest, *in persona Christi,* the person who manifests Christ, who blesses, absolves, and administers Jesus' healing touch.

Even a priest's clothes are sacred, consecrated, a blessing. As is a nun's veil or habit. They're not just symbols, they're sacred. The priest's stole can drive away evil powers. It's all part of the grace imparted to priests to heal people.

In an exorcism, the effect of a sacred presence, a priest or a nun, is to drive devils completely wild, in shock or fear, because they sense this is not just any person, but the presence of God, a person consecrated to God.

People who have a great devotion to Christ in the priesthood have a respect for the vesture and the body of the consecrated. If God came again, would you shake hands with Jesus, or fall on your hands and knees and beg for a blessing?

The Breath of Souls

We have lost this sense of Christ among us, of God among us. We still see moments in certain languages where God is there—*adios, adieu*—until we meet in God. Goodbye is an abbreviated version of God be with you. Like our language, our understanding of the supernatural has gone from something so noble, so lofty, so sublime, so beautiful, to something that is very profane or trite. And so we live in the ordinary. We've lost sight of the fact that when the

Lord created Man He breathed on him, generating the breath of Life.

We also forget how Christ, when He first appeared to the apostles in the upper room, on the day after the Resurrection, in an act of mercy, blessed them. To heal their timidity, to break their stupor, their incredulity, their sins, He breathed the Divine Breath of Life on them.

In an exorcism, there are moments when the devils manifest themselves, and when the priest simply breathes on them, they go into complete, catatonic silence. The breath, the breath of the priest, *(exsufflatio* in Latin), is healing, it's a sacramental. In ancient baptismal liturgies, part of the preparation was to breathe on the child or adult; in that case the priest's breath was sacramental.

I'm suggesting a new perspective here. I'm suggesting that if your faith was as big as a mustard seed, and you understood how to invite the supernatural into your life, you could tell a mountain to move and it would.

If your faith was as big as a mustard seed, there could be more miracles, more dramatic healing in our lives, in our families, no question.

But it starts with a realization of Holy Hands, much like that of the newly ordained priest in Ireland when seeing the suffering woman.

For the seminarians who witnessed that, the experience took them deeper into Eucharistic Adoration, into the role of sacramentals, into their devotional reading, and into a greater understanding that the priest is an agent of mercy, grace, *in persona Christi Capitis,* the person of Christ the Head. They witnessed the authority of Christ, the High Priest, over the devil. It affirms the theological reality, what they can learn through their intellect. In Knock, when they saw the manifestation of the demonic in a tiny woman, they also saw the manifestation of the Divine and how it triumphs over the power of evil. It showed the power of Christ, His victory over Satan. He already has been seen driving away the devil, and the devil is on the run. *"Holy Hands, Holy Hands! It's burning! It's burning, it's burning!"*

A priest who blessed rain gave them great hope. And that's why people sometimes come to places like Our Lady of Knock, because maybe they're indifferent, even contemptuous, and they rediscover the Church—the incarnate sign of Hope. In holy places like Knock, they find hope.

Like the seminarians, I want you, too, to share this great hope. I want the experiences described on these pages to show you the manifestation of the Divine and its triumph over the power of evil, how Christ is present, victorious over Satan, how Christ has driven away the devil and put him on the run.

Through this book, I hope to help you realize this power, and to seize my invitation: to recognize the noble compassion of your priest, and to make the supernatural yours, inviting the transforming power of Christ into your life, in the Age of Mercy, to find the Faith, and the miracles awaiting you.~ΑΩ

Prayer of Invitation

Heavenly Father, grant us the wisdom to appreciate and embrace the supernatural vocation of the ordained ministerial priesthood. Through the Rites of Ordination, the candidate is sacramentally configured *in persona Christi Capitis*. May we realize that he has Holy Hands—the hands of Christ. *Through Jesus Christ, Our Lord,* **Amen.**

"We have no right to rest as long as a single soul is Satan's slave."

~ St. Maximilian Kolbe

Undying Perseverance
Chapter 2

T hink of the words of the Lord's Prayer, the final petition: ... *deliver us from Evil.* This is not an abstraction, but as the Catholic Catechism notes, a *person,* Satan, the Evil One, the angel who opposes God. The devil throws himself across God's plan and the work of salvation accomplished in Christ.

Think of how Christ's ministry begins with temptation, the spirit of evil. Each temptation depicted in the gospels is a temptation away from the Cross. As Servant of God, Archbishop Fulton J. Sheen, said in his talk, "The Demonic Today" *(see fultonsheen.com),* "The temptation away from the Cross is the demonic. The essence of the demonic is the anti-Cross." The demonic is the spirit, without the Cross.

There's no Christ without the Cross! That's your call as a Christian, and more specifically, that's the call of the priesthood—the Cross. Nowhere is the demonic so visible than at the crucified feet of our Savior, who, thought to have been vanquished by the power of evil, has vanquished all powers of darkness, for our Redemption.

In the Incarnation, Christ came to heal the flesh, the elements of the natural world, to "supernaturalize" us. Again, as the Catechism points out, Christ's compassion toward the sick and his many healings of every kind of infirmity are a resplendent sign that "God has visited his people" and that the Kingdom of God is close at hand *(CCC 1503)*. He came, too, to supernaturalize nature and the cosmos. That's why His priests bless the elements, to preempt demonic influence, and to use these elements to impart the power of grace, much like the priest in Knock did with falling rain. This blessing prevents the devil from using natural elements to gain more influence in this world.

The Lord's healing *is* the Cross. There are no shortcuts to Calvary. Remember, healing is a journey. Deliverance from evil, too, starts with commitment, with perseverance. The Cross is the secret to apostolic success and fruitfulness.

Can You Offer a Cross?

When people come to me, for exorcism, to be delivered of evil spirits, I ask: *Are you willing to drink the chalice of the Lord, drink the chalice of His Blood, to be healed?* How badly do you want to suffer and be freed? Those are the Lord's terms. I tell them that I, too, am being crucified, spiritually, the Lord, literally—we are reliving His crucifixion for the salvation of your soul. What can *you* offer? *Can you offer your life on the Cross in the battle against the devil?*

Exorcism and deliverance are the most visually powerful confirmations of the responsibility vested in men ordained by Christ in Holy Orders. Because through these prayers, through this priestly intercession, the enemy is released from the souls of those under siege, and is ordered to the foot of the Cross, as the priest and those assisting him call upon the holy and awesome name of Jesus. They call for the demons to *give place* to Jesus Christ—to *bow down* before God's mighty hand, to *tremble* and *flee*.

It's spiritual warfare, after all. Someone who commands a multitude of evil spirits relishes combat against the power of God. But to drive away even one evil spirit takes more than the armies all nations could assemble to fight terrorism in the world. Do you realize how powerful the *least* demon is? Do you realize what you are asking of God, and of the Church ... of me?

But let me tell you this, too: St. Thomas Aquinas, in his *Summa Theologica,* the section on the angels, reveals how powerful our guardian angel is, and how the lowest angel in Heaven's hierarchy has more power than all the devils from Hell put together. Yes, one angel in glory has the power and grace from God to vanquish all demons! That's why in exorcisms, we call upon guardian angels, and archangels, Sts. Michael and Raphael, to help us battle the enemy.

Also consider St. John Mary Vianney, who rarely did formal, solemn exorcisms, but was a model of spiritual combat. He practiced fasting and mortification, and it was known that his sole sustenance was a potato he ate every now and then. As a parish priest, through Holy Confession, he was able to drive away demons in possessed penitents through prayers of absolution, without recourse to formal rites. During one of Fr. Vianney's many combats with the devil, as described in *The Curé of Ars, Patron Saint of Parish Priests,* by Fr. Bartholomew O'Brien (©1987, TAN Books) the evil one appeared to him as a fiery creature, a monster, and with a finger wagging, told this humble priest: *"How thou makest me suffer! If there were three men on earth like thyself, my kingdom would be destroyed."* After all, here was a priest who, in his lifetime, would hear the confessions of more than *a quarter-million souls.* God blessed his priesthood, but it took six or seven years for the hearts of his parish to turn. (Hearts he could read, by the way, as a gift from God.) Through it all, the devil relentlessly pursued Fr. Vianney, battled him, tempted him.

As Fr. O'Brien wrote, at night, the devil would create noises so loud that this beleaguered priest couldn't sleep. In a fearful voice, he'd cry out: *"Vianney! Vianney! Potato eater! Ah, thou art not yet dead! I shall get thee, all right."*

One night, Fr. Vianney heard horrible sounds. Strange creatures. Roaring lions. Despite his initial alarm, he was overjoyed because he realized by his suffering of the devil's torment there would be "a big fish," many conversions, the next day, conversions so great, people would wait hours, even days, to visit Fr. Vianney in his confessional.

He'd get little sleep. He'd lie in bed for just minutes, to recoup whatever rest he could. The devil set the bed afire. The whole bed frame was in flames, shooting two to three feet in the air. The Curé of Ars quickly took in all these things, and rolled over, muttering in his sleep, "Oh it's you, *grappin.* I don't have time for you just now. I'm tired." And after dismissing the devil as a pest, a varmint, he went back to bed, flames surrounding him.

In Ars, pilgrims can still marvel at St. Vianney's singed bed, a reminder of his skirmishes with the unseen enemy. Can you imagine awakening to flames surrounding you? Even if you were half asleep, the adrenalin would kick in. You'd run. But through smoke and flames and heat, as tired as he was, Fr. Vianney was peaceful, calm; he slept. The supernatural was so common, it became natural. Although he could feel the intensity of the flames, they never touched him. His complete trust in Christ allowed him to be enveloped in the flames of His Sacred Heart.

"With the Name of Jesus we shall overthrow the demons," Fr. Vianney said.

Devils, Retreating in Terror

Knowing I'm an exorcist, people frequently ask me if I'm afraid of demons. No, for who are they compared to the awesome power of God? Why should we fear fallen angels or seraphim and cherubim when Christ liberated souls from legions of evil spirits and we have the Father liberating us from the power of darkness to bring us into Light? I have been privileged to see the absolute power and authority of Almighty God over evil.

My ministry, after all, is the extended apostolic ministry of Christ, bringing the Gospel of Light from darkness. People who've walked in the shadow of the valley of darkness are being set free.

The gospel enlightens, elevates, and frees us from a world that in this age—most exorcists today believe—is even more terrorized by the demonic. But as priests, we're invoking Christ's authority. As priests, we have authority in the name and person of Jesus, through Holy Mother Church. We're able to break the demons' grip and tread on their dominion.

I've seen a woman possessed by hordes of evil spirits, walking up walls and on ceilings. I've seen objects move seemingly of their own accord, and men and women levitating, even as half a dozen men tried to hold them down.

But let me tell you, every bit of that is nothing compared to the Divine Majesty, the healing of a soul possessed, and the love that soul—released from a prison of torment through his priest—has for his Heavenly Father. I will never forget the unspeakable beauty described by a religious sister delivered from years of possession, as she saw her priests battling the powers of darkness, then impenetrable rays of light and all the power of Holy Mother Church, the Divine Mercy, piercing the veil of her own soul.

I was assisting Fr. Giancarlo Gramolazzo, F.D.P., president of the International Association of Exorcists, and two other priests, in the exorcism of the nun, in her early 20s. Her family had made a pact with the devil 300 years ago. It was part of a Satanic rite involving human and animal blood sacrifices that consecrated her family lineage to the devil for 12 generations. During Mass, she'd break out in strange tongues. She often couldn't get out of bed; five people couldn't move her. At times even one of her arms felt like it weighed several hundred pounds. Yet she was a model religious and had a great zeal for the Lord. It was gut-wrenching that she could be affected by a pact made 300 years ago. But the power of the devil is impressive. He's been around for millions of years, no? Three hundred years is nothing to him.

Fr. Gramolazzo was having a tremendous effect on the devils possessing the sister. At one point, they pretended not to hear the prayers. But, led by the Chief Exorcist of Rome, we persisted, and the devil became more furious with our responses and prayers. *"Basta! Basta!"* the devil screamed in Italian. *"Enough! Enough!"* And the woman, in the devil's grip, was clamping her ears so her captors couldn't hear us. *"One at a time! One at a time!"* the devil screamed. *"I can't take this!"* We continued, realizing we were winning the battle.

The possessed woman turned to Fr. Gramolazzo, and in Italian, the devil said: *"If you are such a great exorcist, you don't have the need for the others."* Father looked up and quietly said, "We're all equal brethren here." We continued praying, realizing that the devil was angered by the cumulative power of the priesthood. Soon after, the possessed woman went into a fit—the devil within her was in crisis—and screamed out in pain. He could no longer resist. Together in Christ, we had tremendous power. Through us, Christ was expelling the demon.

After it was over, and the nun came to, she expressed fervent relief. "I could see the torment and the darkness. I could feel it, but I was not there. I couldn't move—a prisoner in my own body." It was as if the motor was on, but the transmission wasn't engaged. A force was moving her body for her.

"I could see the light," she said. "I could see *Christ!* And I could see Christ in all of you. I could understand the mystery of Faith and Christ working in the Church, in the mystery of the priesthood. The devils were retreating in terror. I could hear the Blessed Mother, who with her sons, the priests, represented the mystical body of Christ. Each time you said a prayer, you were bringing me back from the legions of Hell. I could feel the power of Jesus through all of you, the communion of priests, the communion of grace overcoming the devil. It brought such relief! It brought Heaven to my Hell. It seemed I was out of my body. But I could see my soul and the power of the priesthood and its great fruitfulness, and even ecstasy. I was overjoyed, overwhelmed, to see that manifestation of grace, the vision that the Lord enabled me to see!"

Can you imagine?

She could feel the power of Holy Hands! So could the devil. He reacted even to the touch of the priest's stole. It was almost as if it was burning him. But as priests, it wasn't our bodies or hands: It was hands consecrated to bless, and even blessed vestments, that created reaction in the devil.

The experience of exorcism would bring her into a deeper contact with her vocation, and she would grow in holiness and sanctity.

Most holy people journey through in spite of demonic attacks. They have great spiritual *ascesis* (self-discipline). And they also receive great graces of holy love, Divine Love, over weeks, months, and years. They increasingly get holy and sanctified. God permits them to be attacked and possessed to strengthen them, to allow them to grow in more holiness, according to His will.

They're freed and liberated also according to His will in an act of His mercy.

St. Vianney was oppressed, not possessed, for a different outcome, because there are varying degrees of sanctification. For him and other holy men and woman like him, the torment, the obsession of the devil may not have been so much for self-purification, as it is with most sinners, but for sanctification, for reparation of others' transgressions.

Hollywood vs. Heaven: No Contest

If you're a "vampire priest," OK. Hollywood loves you. But Hollywood, even with its anti-Catholic bias, has a grudging understanding of the Church's legitimacy. Hollywood has developed a great market for the demonic, for spirits. Someone I know in Hollywood told me producers wanted to film a "live" exorcism, capturing someone under the force of evil spirits. They sought out representatives of the Roman Catholic Church, but the Church has utmost discretion in these matters. It would never compromise the person possessed, for he or she is a victim and requires protection.

So they called "Fr. Jason," a self-proclaimed Catholic exorcist, really a Protestant minister, who said, "No problem, you can film my 'exorcism.'" So Fr. Jason was there with a person that a team of consulting doctors and psychologists had claimed was demonic. The paranormals and ghost busters were there. Fr. Jason was ready to go.

It was all a misrepresentation, but the producers didn't care. Fr. Jason started commanding the evil spirits to leave the person, but nothing was happening. Suddenly, the devil spoke from the person's mouth: "No, *you* leave. You're wasting time, you phony. You *fake priest*. You *baloney priest.*" This self-appointed exorcist got embarrassed, for he wasn't a priest at all. The devils could see right through him. The devils can see Christ in a Catholic priest but will never see Christ in an imposter priest.

Why is that?

Simply stated, it's because priests act in the person of Christ, to deliver people from evil in communion and obedience to the Church, beginning with its local authority, the bishop. Of course, the bishop doesn't give the priest the power; he gives the priest permission to use the power, a mandate to act in his behalf in a public way to exorcise with Christ's full authority.

The bishop is the moderator of these priestly charisms. The Church's legitimacy and the priesthood's power over demons is recognized over and over in the ministry given to me by the grace of God, and the Church will never lose that, even in this increasingly secular, godless world.

One of the most powerful reminders of that occurred on April 20, 2005, the day after Pope Benedict XVI was elected as our new Holy Father. I was assisting at an exorcism at one of the oldest churches in the world, St. Anastasia's near Rome's Palatine Hill, one of the oldest parts of the city. The church was built under ground when the early Christians were secretly celebrating the Holy Eucharist. Along with two young priests from the United States, I was assisting Fr. Francesco Bamonte of the Servants of the Immaculate Heart of Mary. The possessed was an Italian medical doctor in her mid-40s. The doctor had been involved in a demonic cult that masqueraded as a prayer group. She had night terrors, was choked, thrown out of bed, and had violent fits of rage and blasphemies. She spoke in strange tongues and knew of hidden events. She had the strength of 12 men. For the exorcism, she consented to be restrained, on a chair affixed to a 300-pound metal platform.

During the exorcism prayers, the platform rose off the ground. She spoke in different languages (but knew only Italian). Parts of the ritual are in Latin, but the demon had excellent comprehension of the Church's ancient language. At one point, through the woman, the demon started divulging information about the American priests, only seven years ordained, to try to get them to leave. They ignored him. They kept praying, staying focused on their prayer. Fr. Bamonte ordered the demon to reveal its name, how it had entered the woman, and when it would leave. The demon tried hard to resist. Upon Father's invoking the Blessed Mother's authority, the devil said, *"I'm constrained to be humble."* (Because the devil is proud.) *"If it wasn't for that Woman, I would destroy you all and this creature,"* he said, referring first to the Blessed Mother and then to the woman doctor, the possessed.

Suddenly, the demon started whispering, almost weeping—"See the Woman there? She's here. *She's in our midst.* In this room. *I'm afraid! I'm afraid!* How we've suffered! How we tried in this past age, we from Hell, we wanted to have our own candidate, someone we could use more to our ends on the Throne of Peter. *Do you not know how greatly we are suffering?* Just when we thought we had our own candidate on the Throne of Peter, one most willing to do our bidding, we were stopped by the Woman. *This Woman.* The Pope, like the last, is protected by the Woman."

What great sign do you need when we have testimony from Hell itself, showing God's power, Heaven's protection and the Blessed Virgin's intercession the day after the papal election! *It's overwhelming, to think about it.*

Then, as Fr. Bamonte invoked the Blessed Mother's name to call out the devil, we heard a tremendous wailing out of the woman's mouth and then bloodcurdling screeching and guttural sounds. She was finally freed. That is Christ's power working through His Church, through the ministry of His priests, through the intercession of the Blessed Mother. And no one can take that away—no one.

Hissing in Your Head

The power of Christian love and virtue, persevering in prayer, gives us hope because through it, we'll overcome evil in this world—any Satanic sect or domination or legion. The great demonic spirits, especially of the cherubim and seraphim ranks—higher and more perfect even before the Fall than the archangels—are powerful spirits, and they try to affect priests and religious and married people. Understand that Hell will always send its more powerful forces against the bedrock of our faith and families.

The battle we have is the constant battle within us—our body, our mind, our heart, our emotions. The world we can see pretty much, but how do you discern the devil, his work, his activity? He's invisible. We cannot know his presence directly.

You can only detect Satan when you are in the love of God, especially exemplified in the Immaculate Heart of Mary and the Sacred Heart of Jesus.

So we have to be aware of this spiritual combat. It's real in this world.

We have to be ever vigilant. Because how does the devil insinuate himself? His voice is sneaky; he'll make you doubt and grow resentful: *"Oh, look what you're doing for your son. Look how ungrateful he is. Look at your daughter. She just does whatever she wants."* And he's there hissing, like a serpent, all these ideas into your head, into your imagination. *"Look at your brothers and sisters. They don't really understand you, do they?*

Why don't you just end it all and jump out the window?" Then: thoughts of suicide.

The devil has a million and one deceptions. On sheer intelligence, he cannot be beaten. We could find no other form of protection were it not for God personally intervening. Still, the devil persists: *"Oh, look at you, look how you're so pathetic in your sin. God doesn't love you. God can't forgive you. You know you're going to Hell. You know it. Go ahead, take the drugs! Go ahead, live in adultery. Enjoy it! There's no hope for you. There's no Heaven for you!"*

Sadly, people buy into this. They become spiritually paralyzed. The devil takes them by the hand and leads them merrily to Hell, first-class delivery. But wait! Instead of feeling sorry for yourself, feel sorry for the *Son of God,* who suffered and died for *you!* Let go of the in and occasion of sin and relationships that cause the sin.

If we really love our children, friends, and family, we will persevere in prayer and virtue—for them. Even though we grow tired, we ask the Lord for strength. Overcome with love. True, true love. With love, you can conquer the devil. He cannot stand it. In the face of anger, hate, and recrimination, true love wins people over and keeps the devil at bay, even expels him.

If your hand causes you to sin, cut it off! "It is better for you to enter life maimed than to have two hands and to go to Hell, to the unquenchable fire" *(Mark 9: 43).*

The words of Jesus to us are very clear. *Very clear.* The stakes are high. This is why we have to have this love of God that's able to overcome the devil himself. If our love is not stronger than the devil's determination, we're finished.

Every Heart's Combat

With love, you're secure. You feel a sense of identity, of self-worth. You feel affirmation as a Child of God. You don't care what other people think. You have a vision. You have a strength. You know where you're coming from, and you know where you're going, and you know what you're doing now. You have clarity of purpose. Strength of conviction. With your mind enlightened, you have true knowledge of God. And there's a happiness and joy in you that the world can never give.

That's why the Lord says, even at Holy Mass: "Peace! *Pacis!* Peace! *Shalom!* Peace I give unto you, not as the world gives, but as I give unto you." This is a gift coming from Jesus and the Immaculate Heart of Mary. When this peace is poured into your heart, and your family's heart, it transforms them! And gives birth to new life. And you will no longer be the same. You are different. You are *beloved*.

But we have to *allow* ourselves to be beloved. The hearts of Jesus and Mary, with that of St. Joseph, lead us to our Heavenly Father's heart. And this is exactly what the devil tries to prevent: He drives a wedge between our hearts and those of Jesus, Mary, and Joseph and that of our Heavenly Father. That is where the combat is.

Pope Paul VI said in a Nov. 15, 1972, general audience that the devil is real. The devil isn't a symbol or a figment of the imagination, but a very real being with will, with hatred, with intelligence far superior to anything human.

"We come face to face with sin which is a perversion of human freedom and the profound cause of death because it involves detachment from God, the source of life," Pope

Paul VI said. "And then sin in its turn becomes the occasion and the effect of interference in us and our work by a dark, hostile agent, the Devil.

"Evil is not merely an absence of something but an active force, a living, spiritual being that is perverted and that perverts others. It is a terrible reality, mysterious and frightening. ...Who can forget the highly significant description of the triple temptation of Christ? Or the many episodes in the Gospel where the Devil crosses the Lord's path and figures in His teaching? And how could we forget that Christ, referring three times to the Devil as His adversary, describes him as 'the prince of this world'?

The lurking shadow of this wicked presence is pointed [out] in many, many passages of the New Testament. St. Paul ... warns us of the struggle we Christians must carry on in the dark, not only against one Devil, but against a frightening multiplicity of them. ... Grace is the decisive defense. Innocence takes on the aspect of strength. ... Jesus teaches us this by pointing to 'prayer and fasting' ... the Apostle suggests the main line we should follow: 'Be not overcome by evil, but overcome evil with good.'"

And so we defeat *him*—Evil—with love, with strength, with perseverance.

The story about Luis that follows is an exceptional illustration of a soul's perseverance, of a grace moving, again, over generations, through the sacramental of the Rosary, merited to Luis through God's mercy.

Merit is a gift God gives us through the Pascal Mystery, always relative and in view of His Son's merits, the foundation of our own. Ultimately, merit in itself is impossible, only through Christ, and in this case, through the Blessed

Virgin Mary's intercession. These virtuous actions and favors can open a door, in view of God's mercy, later in life. Virtue, followed by grace conditions God's favor, as well as a person's ability to receive grace.

People who focus their will on coming into close union with the will of Christ are those who have the most success against evil spirits. They embrace a supernatural training discipline to develop supernatural fitness. They build spiritual muscles, follow ascetical practices of mortification, receive the sacraments often, offer up bodily penances, and use sacramentals through piety and devotion.

Luis' story is exceptional in how deliverance occurred, when it occurred, and how spontaneously it occurred. And it all began for him with a "children's game." Typically, people with the worst demonic harassment can require years of spiritual direction under a priest, priests who are hard to find because many dioceses have no exorcists. It takes special priests, too, to support the exorcist.

Luis persevered for decades. When he realized *who* he had invited into the deepest recesses of his soul, he began feeding on Scripture. (St. Alphonsus Liguori says love of the word of God and a zeal for Sacred doctrine is from God. It's holy. God puts a special gift in these souls, and these souls will be led to eternal salvation.) Also, his wife interceded for him through the Rosary.

Luis sought the intercession of St. Pio of Pietrelcina, who bore the wounds of our crucified Savior for 50 years and led a life on the Cross with Christ. Like St. Vianney, St. Pio fully confronted assaults of the evil one who was very present all of the saint's life. As a consequence, the fruitfulness of his ministry is felt even today. So it's no surprise that Luis prayed to St. Pio and begged the Lord for mercy. In time, the Lord heard and delivered him.

Luis Begins His Story

We all have a mystical life. When I was younger, I had visions, dreams. I'd lie in bed at night and before I'd fall asleep, I'd see things, and then sometimes they would come to pass. It still happens, but I do not allow my mind to depend on it, because that can be dangerous.

The greatest gift you can have is to be humble and depend on God. If you look for answers through a medium or through sorcery, you'll be punished, one way or another. God will take your mind away to teach you a lesson.

He taught me well. I spent 40 years in the "wilderness," to learn this lesson: *"I am the Lord your God, you shall have no other gods before me."*

He doesn't share his glory with any other god. When you worship other gods, you're an idolater. This is the worst sin against God.

My father's parents are the ones who kept me alive, through all my years. My wife, Nilda, too. I am 59 now. When I was a child and we were at my grandparents' house, at 7 o'clock every night we prayed the Rosary, all 15 decades that we had at the time. Then at the end, we'd say the Litany of the Blessed Virgin Mary.

If you came to my grandmother's house, you'd better pray and shut up. That's the way my grandfather was. Very strict. He built something in my soul. In later years, I could feel him and my grandmother praying next to me, even though they'd been dead for years. I could hear their voices next to me. Imagine; every night we prayed 15 decades. It was an hour and a half, or an hour and a quarter. My grandfather never backed down. At the end, you had to kiss his hand!

When I was 14, I promised God to be a godly man. I promised to never smoke, drink, or do drugs, and it was the 1960s. I told him I would be holy and pure, and the reason was that I wanted to be a Franciscan Friar. But at 18, my lack of purity contributed to my downfall.

We lived in suburb near Old San Juan, Puerto Rico. We'd moved there when I was 12, and when we moved we had new neighbors and friends. I always was a loner. But I knew in my life I was never alone. When I was young, I had this feeling someone was around me. I never saw this someone, who was good, who watched over me. It was a voice I heard inside my heart and soul.

But when I was 12, after we moved, I met a man across the street I later called "Papa." Because my father and mother always worked, he was like a father to me. He was very smart. He read a lot. But he didn't believe in Christ. He was into Hinduism and yoga. I disagreed with him: "The Bible cannot be wrong. Why don't you believe in Jesus Christ?"

We always played bingo and Monopoly and other board games. One day when I was 16, I noticed some kids playing with a Ouija board. To me, it was a game. I knew nothing about the thing. I bought one and put my hands on it, and by myself, the thing was moving like crazy. I didn't know why it was moving. I asked it questions, stupid questions, and it answered me. I asked the kids across the street if they ever played alone. They said, "That's impossible. It only works with two people." So I kept it to myself. I said nothing. Maybe I am crazy, I thought. But when I put my hands to it, it was like someone was on the other side.

About three or four months after I started playing with the Ouija board, I was in bed. My brother and I shared a room. I was talking to my brother, and the next thing I know, he went running to my mother, probably screaming. I couldn't remember anything. I remember my father and mother waking me up. "You better go to church and start praying!" they said. It must have been only five minutes that passed. The next day, my brother told me: "You were lying on the bed, and then got up and started praising the devil."

I was a person changing slowly. I didn't realize what was going on. Something was pushing me. It wasn't until I got older that I realized it was evil.

Paralyzed by Two Forces

One day, at Papa's house across the street, a lady came over, a very beautiful woman, seven years older than me. She was a medium, a psychic. I was 18 by this time. She said some spirits would like to talk to me. And if I wanted, they would come to me. "What are you talking about?" I asked. But just like she said, it happened two weeks later, when I was at Papa's house. Usually, I'd stay late at night, talking, playing bingo. While I was sitting in the dining room at midnight, a spirit came to me for the first time. My whole body changed. I felt as if something were coming in there. I stood up straight. I could hear, but I could not control my body. I started speaking different languages— then my own language. The spirit started speaking to Papa through me. He told Papa that he was a spirit from someplace, coming from some old time—he was more than 2,000 years old. Papa asked: "What's your name?" "G—," he said. He believed in these things. I had no idea what a medium was. I became a channel for him and didn't know it.

G— was the only name I remember and maybe that's not a typical Indian name, but that's the name I remember, and he was some guru in India. After that, a lot of Hindu gurus would come to me and talk to Papa. Little by little, I became a medium—or at least, that's what I thought I was. Every time Papa wanted to talk to his gurus, I just sat down and right there, they'd talk.

My life changed. I was living within two forces—that's what it felt like. There were times when I felt completely paralyzed. I was like a statue, not moving. My hands changed position. The complexion of my face changed. My voice changed. G— had a low, quiet voice; the others were rough voices, or different voice tones. I would feel their energy around me, but they would not let me move. I could talk, but the energy stayed. I did not know what it was. I'd feel two different things, evil or good. Sometimes, I'd feel pressure on my chest and throat and I couldn't speak. I was frozen.

One day, the lady psychic asked me to meet a medium friend who needed another medium to help her. When we got there, there were six or seven people there. More came later. The people, to me, looked very disturbed—a person's eyes are the mirror of his soul. You could tell they weren't right. My sense was they were full of the demonic. You could feel it. Some were clearly possessed or oppressed. For some reason, I wasn't scared. I could see the evil, but I wasn't scared. I thought nothing would happen to me. The psychic had this charisma. Once I met another woman who told me: "I know this lady is a witch." I said, "You know what, I believe so, but a beautiful witch."

All these people needed spirits to help them. I thought I was helping them. *No way.* In the realm of the spirits, you begin with a little guy. You might think he's helping you, but then the "badder," the heavier spirits, take over. By the time I got into the heavier spirits, the smaller ones were gone, and I was all by myself. I'd go to bed but didn't sleep. I could feel the evil presence in my room. I couldn't do anything. I tried to pray. Nothing worked. I didn't want to sleep in my room anymore. It felt like I was going into a tomb.

One night it was so terrible, there was such a bad feeling around me, I felt like I was going crazy. I was praying, begging God: *Please, send someone, anyone.* Then from out of nowhere, my room lit up with a bright light—the whole room—and I fell asleep like a child. I had been asking God at that moment, I was praying for anyone to come, not necessarily Jesus, but I was so desperate I was calling even Papa because I couldn't go anywhere. I was stuck. I was dealing with something I couldn't handle.

I was desperate, It was like you know in your mind where you're going to go, to Hell, and it was frightening to me. And the bright light shown in my room, brighter than the sun. Then I went out with the lady, and I no longer felt fear. Before, I had felt at least two times like they were going to steal my spirit. My spirit was coming out of my body, but the light was why I could go places with evil with no fear. At the time, I thought the light was from God, but much later, I decided that since the peace didn't last and didn't repent and change, it was another devil's trick.

When the lady psychic said there are spirits of light that shine around you and they want to be in you, it surprised me and touched me. I was weak. Eventually, all the spirits she was using came into me at night. I was dancing like a crazy man and smoking a cigar, even though I hated cigars, because through this spirit and cigar smoke, the psychic could divinize the future.

Many things she said would happen to me did happen. But it wasn't me dancing, it was someone else. At other times, I was almost in a trance. It would last 45 minutes to an hour. I was not in a full trance; this was something different. I was there, but I was not there. My eyes were closed the whole time. I could hear what was said.

I started going with the psychic to different places, to the beach, a river. She'd do her spiritism stuff. She'd do old pagan rituals, no different than satanic rituals. I'd look at her and she changed to the kind of person she had inside of her. She would tell you something and it would come to pass. She was so deep into this that even she didn't know she had the evil one inside. She did not know how dark it was behind her.

I was in the devil's grasp, too. I was right inside his backyard having a picnic with him and I didn't know. Being inside those rituals, doing things these people do, I wasn't there. Deep down I wanted to help people. But when you are dealing with dead people, you're not dealing with godly people. Many spirits visited me. I was a magnet. I would take some of these evil spirits, and at night when I could not sleep, I would pray with them, to see if the spirit

I had with me could be released out of the misery they had. After a while, I said: This is not from God. This is evil. But I still learned things from the spirits. I went to Papa when I was 19 and said, "Papa, this time next year, you'll be dead." I told him I would never talk to him again. And a year almost to the day, he died. I did not go to his funeral, but I cried; he was like a father to me.

A Curse, a Witch, a Priest

I went to a priest. I said, "Father, help! There's evil in me, demonic forces." He said, "Those are temptations." "Father, you don't believe in Satan?" I asked. "*Cuento de hadas,*" he said—fairytales. "The devil does not exist." I wondered to myself how he could say the devil does not exist. Jesus is wrong? He said, "Do not worry about those things." So I had a small Confession. I hardly ever received Holy Communion after that. I didn't want to. I felt dirty inside. I knew that .from my childhood, I was not worthy to receive Him.

When I was 21, a year before I got married, I was driving in my car and I saw an accident—it was my brother! I saw him on the ground. His face was full of glass. He was covered with blood. His car hit an electric pole, right in the center of the car. The engine was slammed to the back of the car, that's how bad it was. People at the accident said he was dead. I said he's not dead, he's my brother! I was crying out to God: *Please wake him up!* When we got to the hospital, 15 minutes later, he woke up.

That same week, I had an accident. The women psychic had a problem with her car, and asked if I could help her out. I told her I would, but didn't want to deal with this evil anymore. I was using gas to wipe off part of the car. By mistake, I touched the battery and caught fire. I caught fire on both my hands, especially my right hand. I rolled over to extinguish the fire. The car also caught fire.

In my hospital room that night, there was a witch running around the room, and she was laughing at me. I said, "God, this is it. I'm not afraid of evil anymore." When the medium lady came to visit, I asked, "There is a witch running around. What for?" She said someone had tried to put a curse on her car so she'd have an accident, and I took it instead. I never talked to her again. The time she came to see me in hospital was the last time I saw her.

Right there, I said: *I will not call on the spirits anymore.*

The doctor told me my right hand was bad. He could not guarantee whether the hands would make it. There was no skin. You could see veins. This was 1971; they didn't know how to heal a third-degree burn. My hands were swollen four to five times normal size.

The doctor said, "You might lose your hands, because of infection." I told him I would not lose my hands. (I saw my hands, in the future, and that had not happened.) The doctor was worried, but just like I told him, in a week, the skin had healed, and I grew hair on it. He told me he had never seen anyone heal so quickly. After two weeks, I was out, and my brother was well and out one week later.

I started running away from this thing. I wanted to end my life. But I said, this is wrong. I tried to keep my mind busy. I barely slept three or four hours a night for many, many years. I got up at 3 o'clock every night for months. If I had nightmares, it would be around that time.

I went through my life, in chains. I married my wife, Nilda, on Dec. 22, 1972. We had five sons. So I still prayed. When they were going to get in trouble, I knew. As they got older and into more serious trouble, I'd pray. Once, in the middle of the night, the voice in my heart and soul told me to pray for my son, who wasn't home. I prayed 45 minutes. My son later told me he was caught with his friends by a gang in an alley. One boy started shooting at him. They jumped into a car and took off. The boy in the front seat was hit by a bullet and died. My son said he usually rode in the front seat; that was the only time he hadn't. No bullets touched him.

To keep busy, I started painting. God gave me this gift. People even bought my paintings. I traded a portrait for a saxophone and a flute, and I started learning to play on my own. I loved it. I taught myself how to read music. I learned to keep busy. I painted for hours and hours until I got ex-hausted. I reproduced a famous painting from an old Bible of Jesus preaching and healing the sick, but I never finished painting the left side. I was going to put myself in there. Over many years, I could see my face in there, searching for God. This was my desire. But I could never finish it. I still haven't.

I always worked a couple of jobs to keep my mind busy, and painted at night. Yet I had evil thoughts, even to destroy my children and other loved ones. Is that from God or the devil? *Imagine, destroying your own children?* My wife knew something was wrong with me. At night, the spirits would come and take me over and she could hear the voices.

It was like having something on my mind that I couldn't get rid of—anger and hate—and not forgiving anyone. This is what I had on my mind 24 hours. I couldn't take it anymore.

In 1983, I went into a deep depression. I destroyed my house two times, with a baseball bat, totally destroyed my house. The kids were running. I told my wife to go back to Puerto Rico (we were living in the United States by then) and she went for six months. I walked around my house and I cannot mention the evil thoughts that were in my mind. I lived alone. I was a sinner many times over. I did things I did not want to do, things that I cannot tell except to my confessor.

I put myself in the hospital. I said, "Doctor, I feel like I want to kill someone." The doctor said, "Nothing is wrong." I said, "You are wrong, blind, only God can help me with what I have." They put so many drugs in my body it was shaking. I was like a zombie for months. They couldn't figure anything out. At home, I felt the same anger.

When I went into the hospital, my wife turned to the Blessed Mother and prayed from her heart the Rosary for the first time. She committed herself to the Blessed Mother, for me and my family.

She still prays the daily Rosary. That was what kept me sane, until the time of my deliverance. I lost my job, and I couldn't work anymore. I went back to school for computer programming, and got honors. I tried to keep busy again.

The devils made me do more things I didn't want to do. I would cry. It's evil that takes over, and we are a puppet for the evil one. I began to understand that God allowed this all these years to teach me a lesson, for I was an idolater.

Photographed by Sylvester Markowski.

"*Come Unto Me*" by Danish artist Carl Heinrich Bloch,
reproduced in oil on canvas by "Luis," but never finished.

Jesus is the Lord

One night, lying in bed, at the time when I'd get these half-asleep visions, I saw the spirit of Papa, and I said, "What are *you* doing here?" He said, "I came to tell you this: Jesus is the Lord." And he disappeared.

I got out of bed and started reading the Bible for the first time—my wife has books, saints, all over the house. This was a Douay-Rheims Bible. Of all the Bibles I have, in this one God's word is especially true for me. I pray before I open it and ask God to speak to me. And this time, I asked, please give me some-thing so that one day I'm not so angry.

I read Proverbs 24:17-20: *"When thy enemy shall fall, be not glad, and in his ruin let not thy heart rejoice; Lest the Lord see, and it displease Him, and He turn away His wrath from Him. Contend not with the wicked, nor seek to be like the ungodly; For evil men have no hope of things to come, and the lamp of the wicked shall be put out."*

I read in Kings 1, in the King James version (1 Chronicles 10:13, in Catholic RSV), how after Samuel became a prophet and anointed Saul the first king of the Jewish state, Saul went to a witch lady when Samuel died to call the prophet's spirit. And he came, and he told Saul: *You are not supposed to do this.* And God took his kingdom and gave it to David; *Saul was slaughtered.*

I studied God's word, the Bible, for six, seven years. Whatever time I had, I spent on the Book. Whenever I read it, I saw how God works in people's lives. When I picked up the Bible, I still couldn't understand what was happening in my life, what was wrong? When I started reading the Old Testament and St. Paul's letters, it was like the Holy Spirit was breaking me down, showing me what I did wrong. In Isaiah 42:8, God said very clearly, "I am the LORD, that is my name; my glory I give to no other ... " I read this in Leviticus and Exodus, too. I said: *This is God talking, to me!*

St. Pio Intercedes

As I went to different churches, I experienced this new way of praising God, in different tongues, but it seemed more like babbling, and I felt sorry for those babbling. There seemed to be more demons there, and they were supposedly speaking in tongues. But when the Holy Spirit speaks, He does not babble words. †

If you read Acts of the Apostles, in chapter 19, you find that an evil spirit will just not run away because you use the name of Jesus. You have to have the authority of genuine faith. In Acts 19:13-19, sons of a Jewish high priest were exorcizing using Jesus' name. But the evil spirit answered: "Jesus I know, and Paul I know; but who are *you?*" And the man with the evil spirit leaped on them, and overpowered

---

† **Author's note:** I am relating Luis' testimony here. One needs to seriously discern between what is an authentic gift of tongues and what is inauthentic, and perhaps even demonic. According to the Catechism of the Catholic Church (CCC 2003), "Grace is the first and foremost gift of the Spirit who justifies and sanctifies us. ... There are furthermore special graces, also called charisms ... sometimes ... extraordinary, such as the gift of miracles or of tongues—charisms are oriented toward sanctifying grace and are intended for the common good of the Church. They are at the service of charity which builds up the Church." The Catechism cites 1 Corinthians 12 on this point: "To each is given the manifestation of the Spirit for the common good. To one is given ... the ability to distinguish between spirits, to another various kinds of tongues, to another, the interpretation of tongues."

them, so that they ran out of the house naked and wounded. They had not been authorized to do that. Demons know who you are and if you're authorized.

I found one of my wife's books, a book on St. Pio, *Padre Pio: The Wonder Worker*. It talked about how the devil was trying to trick him, and appeared to him in the form of the Blessed Virgin Mary and other saints. He was in a state of confusion, because it was so vivid, and the devil appeared to him as many other things, but he was not that person. He called it the "war against Satan." I said you know what, this Holy Man of God was done worse than me. And if God can do this, allow this, in a man of God, then me, a sinner, he can rip up quickly. Here is Father Pio, a saint, and I am a sinner. And he went through the devil's tricks. He went through a very confused time, but God allowed this for a greater understanding of His grace. I thought of my last temptation in my house, before I picked up the St. Pio book: I wanted to destroy all the Bibles. I got two statues, one of St. Francis hugging Jesus on the Cross and one of the Blessed Mother. I was going to destroy them with a hammer.

But I didn't. I continued reading St. Pio's book, and praying for his intercession for months. One night as I read in my kitchen, I started crying and crying. I felt this man's holiness and I felt so grateful. How many times had I cursed my life? How many times had I asked God to take it away? Every weekend, I didn't want it. The hate, the bitterness, the "no forgiveness for nobody." I couldn't stop crying. I swore to St. Pio that if he would help me, I would honor him the rest of my life. I would grow a beard so that when I got up in the morning and looked in the mirror, I would think of him and Jesus. And I would keep the beard until I died.

Three days later, I was listening to Drew Mariani on Relevant Radio in my car on the way to work, and, Father, you and another priest were on the air, answering callers' questions. I thought: I have to see that priest—I had to see *you*. Maybe this is it. I learned you were going to be in my area the very next weekend.

Delivered from Bondage

I'd been to many priests, preachers, and people praying over me, and putting their hands on me—nothing. At your talk on Spiritual Warfare, sponsored by Relevant Radio in Chicago Heights, when you started praying the Prayer of St. Michael, and the prayers of deliverance, I felt as if the whole building started moving.

I never experienced anything like that in my life. I was standing on my feet and my whole body was moving around me like a tornado. In my mind, I heard an evil voice: "Anytime you go to the floor, crawl like a snake." I said: *No!*

I was looking around. I was asking myself: *Can anyone see what's going on here?* I could feel vibrations in the wall. I couldn't move. It was like I was tied up in my feet. There was twisting around in my chest. I looked at people next to me: *Can you feel **this**?* Then I closed my eyes: *This is it; this is what's going to happen.* My feet were still, but my body was moving around and around. For what seemed like a long time. Father, when you prayed that prayer, I wondered: *People, do you not feel what he is doing? Don't you feel God's presence here?* When I was swirling, I prayed: *Dear God, take* *this away!* Until this thing came out of me! I felt like it came out of my *soul!*

And I started laughing. I felt so happy! I opened my eyes and suddenly I saw a chubby priest standing next to me. Maybe he thought I was going to fall down. "Father, did you see this?" I asked. He just smiled at me. I said again, "Father, this priest touched my spirit!" I asked him where you were, Father Machado, but he did not know. I could not see you that night, Father, but I said, one day I would.

After all I experienced in my life, finally, just like it came into me 40 years ago, it came out from inside.

It was Nov. 22, 2008.

I felt peace I never felt since I was a child.

Confession in Kenosha

Life is not the same. I feel like I am 17 years old again. I have no resentment. How many times I put on the light at night when I felt the evil around me in my mother's house. Now it's like a big weight is out of my life.

I was so grateful, but I still did not go to Holy Communion. I wanted to see you, Father, for Confession. And five months later, at a mission at St. James the Apostle church in Kenosha, Wis., I went to Confession with you. That is secret between you and me but when I saw you preaching, or talking to me, it was like a picture I'd seen of St. Pio in ecstasy with the Holy Spirit, the way your eyes were, and I knew you were searching me, searching me, your eyes blinking, looking deep, deep, into my soul.

I was in Confession with you for an hour and a half. And the day before, at the healing service, you blessed me, with holy oil and the Holy Spirit. It's was like a seal, a relief of this evil thing, and then an anointing—this is not going to happen anymore. When you touched me that day, and anointed my head and hands, I felt with this seal, the evil is no more.

I was so grateful to have you in my life; it has been the blessing of my life. Finally, I found someone who understands me and my problem. You were so humble. I loved you with a special love from the first time I met you. For me to love a person is something;

I have always pushed people away from me. I called my mother, crying, saying, "Mother, God sent me, after 40 years, a holy man in my life!" She had seen me go from a happy young man to a man cursing his own mother, which is evil. The Bible says honor your father and mother and it will give you a long life. That's a gift from God. I cried. I didn't want to hurt anybody because I know what I am inside.

I had been ready to go to Hell, and now I was not.

I forgave all the people I hated and had anger toward. I called them and I asked for forgiveness and I blessed them on top of that. I called people I was angry with, and I said I was sorry and wanted to give them a blessing from God.

I was 18 when the spirits went into me. The Ouija board was the key that opened the door; everything happened after that, one thing after another. But it was my many wrong decisions that brought me so much pain.

I was 58 years old when the spirits came out, the same way they went in. It was 40 years. Like in the Old Testament. I was like the Jews in bondage.

Like Joshua and Caleb.

Now I am looking into joining the (layman's) Third Order Franciscans, and I'm taking Bible study with a priest, and Latin classes. The Mass is in Latin. I want to study Greek, so I can read the Bible in the original texts. I am painting again!

But as it says in Luke 11:24, when a spirit leaves a man, it can return. If the spirit is gone, and he returns to your house (that person's body) and finds the place swept and in order (the person is changed, everything's good) but the person does not pray and keep the house holy, then the spirit comes back with more evil, much worse than its own.

If you leave Jesus out of your life, demons are going to enter your body. I searched everywhere, and Jesus was not entering into my heart. I was fighting, but not fighting with the right answer. Now I know the right answer. Padre Pio became just like Jesus. All his life he was crucified and living in agony every day for 50 years. That's part of being holy, the suffering. This battle never ends.

What I went through with you, Father, was the greatest experience of my life. I do not feel demons inside me anymore. My wife does not hear anything at night. I am sensitive and can I can feel them, the attacks. But it's not possession; it's oppression. I pray the Rosary, pray with St. Michael, with St. Pio, and I can sleep at night, when before I couldn't sleep for years. But now I get up at 3 o'clock to pray.

When you try to be good, it seems like you have to fight with the whole world, not the world itself, the other world, the spirit world. But now it is outside me. That's why I read the Bible. We Catholics should do more, to study God's word. That tells you how to think and act when those things happen. St. Paul says in Ephesians: The battle is not with the flesh and blood, it is with evil. The will of God is the armor and the righteousness. If we don't study the Book, we're lost.

This other world we cannot see is more real than the world we live in. It *is* another world; people do not believe it. But it is so real, if people were truly aware of it, they would not deal with the wrong things sometimes. The battle is around our children, and it's not a one-day shot. It's the rest of our lives.

We are still experiencing challenges in my family, but I struggle and fight and pray. And one day, God will do his work. St. Pio's battles were every day to the day he died.

Should mine be any different? ~ ☽

✝

Prayer for Remedy
of Diabolical Possession or Oppression

Lord Jesus Christ, you came down from Heaven to Earth into the Sacred Womb of Our Lady. You came to snatch us from Satan's tyranny at so great a price, to crush the head of that ancient serpent, to cast him and his fellow apostate angels into the everlasting fire of Gahenna. Have mercy on all those struggling in the clutches of Satan and in those of his infernal legions. Oh St. Michael, glorious prince of the Heavenly Host, lead the cherubim and seraphim, dominations and thrones, the whole nine choirs of angels, into the battle for my soul. May the princes of darkness retreat in fear from the sign of the Most Holy Cross. Through the most holy names of Jesus and Mary, may the gates of Hell be shaken. May demons be flung trembling, headlong, into the pits of Hell. May the Heavens, oh Lord, sing praises to your endless glory and omnipotence. May the joyous celestial choir of the communion of Saints herald the decisive victory of the Lamb of God who takes away the sins of the world and conquers the devil in his pride. *Through Jesus Christ, Our Lord,* **Amen.**

Prayer for Thanksgiving After Deliverance

I thank you, oh Lord, as you have delivered me from diabolical bondage. In the Gospel, with a word, you rebuked and expelled demons, who immediately left those once possessed, now set free. I give thanks with all your Church to the splendors of your majestic power. Oh, Good Shepherd, though I walked in the valley of the shadow of death, with demons inexorably tormenting me, you constantly comforted me. Oh, Blessed Virgin Mary, along with St. Joseph—Terror of Demons, through divine mandate, you've cast into Hell Satan and all his demons who inflicted upon me numerous sufferings. Oh, patron Saints and guardian angels, you have bound all of Satan's specters and cast them into the lake of fire and brimstone. Here on Earth, and one day in the company of the angels, may I praise your name, oh Lord, in eternity forevermore. *Through Christ, Our Lord,* **Amen.**

"The sin of the century is the loss of the sense of sin."

*~ Pope Pius XII, in a 1946 address to the
U.S. Catechetical Congress*

Complete Trust

Chapter 3

Time passes, and graces life, each precious moment blessing. It represents the treasure of eternity—eternal life—with everything in the balance. We need to use time carefully, for it passes so quickly. And the most rewarding way to make sure you don't waste any of your precious moments is to use them to begin your life anew.

How? By trusting in God's Divine Mercy. "Though your sins are like scarlet, they shall be as white as snow; though they are red as crimson, they shall become like wool" *(Isaiah 1:18)*.

The Lord said to St. Faustina that in this Age of Mercy, the only hope for mankind is His mercy. In a paraphrase from her Diary (© 2007, Marian Press), He said to her: *Tell miserable man, wretched man, that I will find solutions to his problems. Tell him to plunge himself into the infinite abyss, the infinite ocean of my Divine Mercy. And there, he will find renewal and strength. There, he will find life I will give him. Let him approach with greatest confidence the Tribunal of Mercy, Holy Confession. When he approaches the confessional, know this, that I Myself am waiting there. I am only hidden by the priest, but I Myself act in his soul. Here the misery of the soul meets the God of mercy.*

Following a confession contritely given, we can hear no sweeter words than these: God, the Father of mercies, through the death and Resurrection of His Son, reconciled the world to Himself and has sent the Holy Spirit among us for the forgiveness of sins; through the ministry of the Church may God give you pardon and peace, and I absolve you from your sins, in the name of the Father and of the Son and of the Holy Spirit.

But wait. The priest who says this is just another man you say? The Pope, our Holy Father, is just another man? What about Jesus? Is He "just another man," too? If you can't see Jesus in the Sacraments, you're wasting His time and your time. If you, a wretched sinner, believe Jesus, the Pope and the priest are just men, guess what? Jesus can't forgive you, either.

What about Holy Communion? If the priest is *just a man,* what are you receiving, bread? What are you coming for if Jesus is *just a man?* Why are you coming to have your children baptized? Is Jesus Christ really the Living Water? Holy Communion is the True Presence—the Body, Blood, Soul and Divinity of Jesus Christ—so who is present? You can say all the words you'd like to bread, to *just a man.*

But what about the holy and awesome power of Christ, humbled in the form of bread and wine? Or in the humble form of a priest, whose ordination has transformed him so that he may receive wretched mankind's sins, absolving them to carry them to the altar as another Christ.

Resist in Faith

Still doubt the power of the priest and Confession?
Consider this: St. John Bosco and St. John Mary Vianney
were known to have healed people of demonic possession
during a good Confession. In the confessional, they relieved
people of evil disturbances.

Behold the mercy of God!

The devil hissed to Fr. Vianney in the confessional: *"I
am with you here, Vianney."* For Lucifer knows the power of
the Sacrament of Penance. The devil will fight you to
prevent a good, full, vital Confession. The distance of a few
feet to the confessional can be the longest path of your life.
But if you don't go, if you receive Holy Communion in a
state of sin, the devil loves that. Can you allow yourself to
receive Holy Communion as sacrilege? Satanists do it for
that reason. Will you?

You cannot escape sin. You can, however, escape the
compounded wounds of sin.

When you see families, wounded, it doesn't mean
everyone's possessed. But every family experiences some
demonic harassment, even if it's "only" temptation. There's
not a single family without some demonic disturbance
through temptation, some disturbance or episode in each
family member's life. It's spiritual warfare after all. It's a
battle against an invisible empire, spirits in the air, and an
empire of darkness. Pope Paul VI, in *Resistite fortes in fide,* on
June 29, 1972, said, in essence: *Remain strong and firm against
the devil. He's prowling about. Remain strong. The devil, who is a
coward, will give up.* If the devil tells you he hates you, don't
care. Just tell the coward to go back to Hell. You're done
with him. If your mother or spouse tells you "I hate you" or

"I don't love you anymore," that hurts, especially the first time. You're shocked? Why? What happened?

Just recall how many times Jesus forgave His enemies. Remember His Passion, what He went through, and what He said: *"Father forgive them; for they know not what they are doing"* (Luke 23:34).

Maybe those who crucified Christ really *do* know what they're doing, but Jesus is saying, "I'm not going to hold on to it. I'm not going to be embittered by it." *Vengeance.* He's refusing to be vengeful. Others may be punished for their sins against you, but *you* don't have to be, by adding bitterness. This is the attitude and heart of Jesus Christ—His love. But He goes beyond that love.

Remember what He told His apostles during His Passion: *"Truly I tell you, one of you will betray me."* St. Peter signaled St. John: "Who?" And Jesus said, *"The one who has dipped his hand into the bowl with me will betray me"* (Matt 26:21-23). Basic etiquette called for the elder to go first, to dip into the dish.

What does Judas do? He dips first because he is blinded by his own passions, his own selfishness. He's feeling nervous because he had just come from the chief priests. The 30 silver pieces, the price of a slave, weigh heavy in his money pouch. And he is leaving the meal hurriedly to complete his betrayal plans. But what does Jesus pray after the meal? *"Holy Father, protect them in your name that you have given me, so that they may be one, as we are one. While I was with them, I protected them, and not one of them was lost except the one destined to be lost, so that the scripture might be fulfilled"* (John 17:11-12). Jesus is speaking of Judas, the son of destruction ... *"It would have been better for that one not to have been born,"* than to betray God Himself *(Mark 14:21)*. This is important. Every time we commit mortal sin, we betray God Himself, like Judas did. Every time we receive Communion in mortal sin, we commit sacrilege. We break God's heart. It's betrayal, plain and simple.

But despite it all, look at our Lord. Look into His eyes, like Peter did after his own betrayal. Jesus is willing to forgive us *anything* ... as long as we come to him with fully contrite hearts.

Think of one of the Church's greatest saints, Saul, who, until he was knocked off his high horse, was a murderer, leading persecutions of early Christians. *"While they were stoning Stephen, he prayed ... 'Lord, do not hold this sin against them.' When he had said this, he died. And Saul approved of their killing him"* (Acts 7, 8). And yet, with a fully contrite heart and firm purpose of amendment, Saul transforms through Christ into Paul, St. Paul. And through his letters, he establishes one of the greatest treatises of our Faith, grounded in love: "Love is patient; love is kind; love is not envious or boastful or arrogant or rude. It does not insist on its own way; it is not irritable or resentful; it does not rejoice in wrongdoing, but rejoices in the truth. It bears all things, believes all things, hopes all things, endures all things" *(1 Cor. 13:4-7)*.

He is speaking of the merciful heart of Christ, of God Himself, lived out in us. But how did Saul arrive at that place? Through recognition of his sins, the laying on of hands by a disciple of Christ, Ananías, and an amended life. We must do the same.

I remember the case of a man who came to Holy Confession and began by saying, "Father, I'm separated from my wife. I know we're married in the eyes of Church, and I ask for forgiveness, but I'm involved with another person."

I asked if the "other person" was married. "Yes, but she's separated, too, from her spouse. And we have feelings for each other. And I'm sorry about that." I said I know you're sorry about that. Now what do you *do?* You have to break free of this relationship. "But we have feelings for each other," he protested. I said I know, but I cannot give you absolution. How can you expect God to forgive you if you say you're sorry but you keep sinning? Remember what Jesus said to the adulterous woman? He didn't say, "I forgive you. Go and sin *some* more." He said, "I forgive you—go and sin *no* more." Jesus called a sin a sin, and He was giving this woman a second chance not to go and sin more and more and more.

But here was this fellow, trying to avoid looking into the eyes of Truth, who is Christ. But before I could share a brief moment of prayer with him, the devil shook him, and he was gone. He blurted out: "OK, thank you, Father, God bless you, goodbye." He was gone. It was like the devil already had a hold on him before he came in to receive the Sacrament of Penance. I was sensing that. No absolution was given. Nothing.

Why? Because he couldn't give up his sin.

St. Alphonsus Liguori said sins of being unchaste are difficult for sinners to renounce, except with special graces from the Lord. This is true even with dying people who are divorced and remarried and are trying to reunite with the Church before their last breath. Basically they have to admit that the person they've considered themselves married to for the last 20 or 30 years isn't really their husband or wife.

They've been living in adultery, objectively speaking. That's a big shock, especially when someone is in the last phases of an incurable disease.

But their *soul* is at stake! How far are they willing to go to change? Are they sad enough for their sin? Are they too sad for themselves to give up their sin?

They pity themselves: *Woe is me. I have feelings for this person.* OK, in Hell you can tell that to the devil, too, that you have feelings for this person. You can feel sorry for yourself in Hell. That's what all the devils do—feel sorry for themselves. And for their sin. And they're hardened in their sin.

Our Father's Embrace

But it's not just laypeople who hesitate to approach the confessional.

A priest I knew never liked Holy Confession. And he had been a priest almost 45 years. Before his ordination anniversary, a benefactor told him that for his 45th year of the priesthood, he wanted to send the priest on a Curé of Ars pilgrimage to the shrine of St. Mary Vianney, now patron of all priests.

In the church sanctuary in Ars, this elderly priest met the shrine's rector, who told him, "Come. I want to show you something." It was a wooden box. "This is the confessional where the Curé battled the devil, where he was able to absolve a quarter-million souls. Would you like to sit here a couple of moments?"

The visiting priest sat down. Immediately he felt something. A heat came over him. He sat there a few minutes, praying and praying. "I feel like a new person," he said when he left the confessional.

Like St. Paul after his encounter with the risen Christ on the Damascus road, this priest was a changed man. He was blind and now could see. His heart softened. Even though he was a priest, he had never wanted to hear Confessions. He deeply feared the confessional. But after that experience, he spent hours and hours there. He completely turned around, praised be to God.

And this is why I write about the devil and how he can influence laypeople and religious alike, especially when it comes to Holy Confession, the greatest obstacle to Evil's hold on wretched man. This is what the devil is like, and what he does to us. How we lose our sense of penance, or remorse. He wants you to prefer your sin. He wants your heart to become hardened to the hearts of Jesus Christ and the Blessed Mother.

So people fall into sin. That's why we have to pray for the grace of God. If we don't pray for these poor souls—perhaps your spouse, your child, your father, mother, brother, sister—they'll go to Hell.

What did the Blessed Mother urgently tell us at Fatima and Lourdes? She said to pray for poor sinners who are going to Hell. She said most sinners go to Hell for lust and being unchaste, and those sins are more prevalent today than 90 years ago.

We can't stop praying for each other in the world. The poor souls, the lives of many souls, are counting on us.

It's a great battle against Satan here. Our battle is against an implacable foe, a wiley adversary who knows no rest Night and day, every moment, the demons work. If you could only see them, how present they are. And yet, when people overcome those demons, the grace that Christ imparts is unbelievable.

I'm extremely moved when I see this type of contrition —when people come to the Lord as the Prodigal Son and really understand and embrace what our heavenly Father offers the sinner. These people understand that He knows they made a journey in time from a dissolute life to a life of amendment and have taken a profound leap of faith, full of supernatural sorrow and contrition. The contrition may be from the type of sin and the objective malice of the sin, or from the person's horror of the sin, even venial sin, horror that caused a life-changing, life-transforming, supernatural contrition—this is what moves my priestly heart.

But getting to that point requires humility, which is really a sense of subjecting oneself to God's authority and judgment. Ultimately, it is obedience and seeking to do God's will above all else, above one's own will.

Obedience is the response of humility, the fruit of humility. Humility feeds all the virtues. Humility is seeing all our failings before the perfection and omnipotence of God Himself, the greatness of God. We realize how relative and insignificant we are before Him. If we are anything of value, it's only through His power and mercy. If you submit to the judgment of Christ, the Son of God, in humility, you will not have to worry about condemnation later. But if you run, your sin will catch up to you.

The Lord told St. Catherine of Siena: *"You are nothing. I am everything. Whatever you are is for me."* Do we live with a full understanding of those words? Ponder them.

A Soul Like a Child's

There are only two reasons people don't go to Holy Confession: Laziness and pride. And yet, when you turn to the lives of two of the greatest religious figures of our time, Pope John Paul II and Mother Teresa, you see in their lives one constant: Daily Confession. With Mother Teresa, there was such a supernatural grace and virtue in her soul, a supernatural love, that it would carry over into the confessional—she would bring her childlike spirit and humility to her confessor.

The cardinal secretary to Pope John Paul II, Cardinal Stanisław Dziwisz, once told me that as our Holy Father lay dying, Cardinal Dziwisz witnessed a desire for the Sacrament of Confession powered by the pope's firm belief in Divine Mercy, to grow in supernatural grace and virtue even as he passed into the next life. It was so great that the Holy Father would emerge from his coma for a few moments each day and call for his confessor. It was extraordinary.

Pope John Paul II would somehow rouse himself, almost miraculously it seems. He would come out of this coma, confess, and then slip back into a coma. On his last day, April 22, 2005, he confessed in the morning. By evening, he called for his confessor again. But by the time Padre Davide, O.S.A., arrived, the Holy Father had passed away. We may presume, in that instance, his desire for the Sacrament of Penance had some form of efficacy. Like Baptism of desire, it's analogous to a Confession of desire, according to classic moral theologians.

So if Mother Teresa felt she needed to go to Holy Confession each day, and Pope John Paul II, in a coma on his deathbed, had received the sacrament daily and still felt the need to go to Confession twice on the day he passed into eternal life, what's preventing you from humbling yourself before your parish priest?

Along with our reluctance to attend Confession, we, as Catholics, sometimes take too much for granted. When our attitude extends to taking God for granted, it interferes with our attempts to save our souls. You can say 'I know God,' but can you explain the elements of how you know God, how He is judging you? On what basis does God hold what is important? What is His Divine Will? How are you seeking His will? How do you resolve all this within your conscience?

When we do not have a proper relationship with God, everything is muddled in our minds, and many Catholics today aren't clear.

They're not clear on the teaching of the Church. They have no clear action in pursuing God the Father, God the Son, God the Holy Spirit. They have no clear understanding of the rapport we need with Holy Mother Church. In seeking His mercy, you must have clarity—plus conviction, purpose, and fortitude—the elements necessary to discover God's plan for you.

You must also understand that Catholicism is not a feel-good religion and feel-good philosophy. We're pursuing absolute commitment, an abandonment to God's will in the person of Christ, Our Lord, who preached to us the Cross, its mystery, its logic, and intellectual power. The Word made manifest in the crucified Savior, His Most Precious Blood in His Sacrifice—Priest, Altar, and Victim.

Last Things

When we perceive the power of Christ, we can see His Divine Mercy, His Sacred Body and Living Water, the Precious Blood and Living Water that flows from His Loving Sacred Heart. St. Thomas Aquinas, St. John of the Cross, and St. Teresa of Avila—all said the more we keep in tune with Holy Mother Church, the more we live God's will, the more it is pursued by God through us. Divine Mercy is made manifest through us.

We can arrive there through something simple: By understanding how to make a good Confession. The greatest way we can experience God's mercy is through Holy Confession—having the proper disposition to entertain and seek its fruits, to see the mystical life poured forth from Confession, its role, and the interaction through a priest who acts as judge. Yes, you're being judged. A sentence is pronounced. There is punishment or remission given. This is a judicial forum. It's also medicinal. The Divine Physician, the Divine Healer, is there.

When you decide to seek Christ through His ministry of Confession, do you know how to prepare yourself? Are you praying for your confessor? And for great grace? This doesn't happen by accident. You have to prepare. To those who seek and prepare for that grace, grace is given.

In St. Alphonsus Liguori's *Preparation for Death,* which if you read, you will never see the priesthood in the same way. You learn you'll always reap rewards for honoring the priesthood. There is a special reward. You will not die without receiving the Last Sacraments, and God will always provide for all who have a special love and respect for priests. The Lord does not forget His own. As he said to Moses and Aaron, "Those that curse you, I will curse; those that bless you, I will bless."

In the story that follows, Mary learns all that God has in store for her through the glory of the priesthood, something she treasures deeply now and that will not go unrewarded.

Mary, over years, recognized that Satan pitted her against sizable obstacles in her life, obstacles that required her to look at herself in the pure light of Christ over and over—through clarity, conviction, purpose, and fortitude. Through Holy Confession, she reaped great fruit. She didn't feel sorry for herself, although sometimes she felt that, too. But through a persisting, systematic way of examining her conscience in humility, a new understanding of prayer, and the gentle but firm guidance of her confessors—many priests over time—she found new life in Christ.

Though her sins were like scarlet, He made them as white as snow—she felt like a child again. Mary learned that "unanswered prayers," prayers that seemingly go unheard because of the wrong intention, motivation, or discernment in what is asked, aren't really unanswered.

It's what we ask, how we ask, when we ask. It may not be the right time, or it's in God's time, for what we're asking may not be in harmony with God's will. The motive of our heart may not be right. If we don't have good intentions, we can't expect God to answer. The way it's answered and how it's answered may not be what we've expected, or may not be prepared for, let alone anticipated. Or, it does come; we just don't see it. So now, each week, Mary prays intimately with Christ, examining her conscience through the Open

Heart of Our Lord, in Eucharistic Adoration. She's in love with Christ. She is not afraid to step into His infinite abyss of Divine Mercy. Through the Sacraments, the gifts He gave us, especially Holy Confession, Mary has learned to always turn to Him first.

Mary Begins Her Story

Mary   God is so real. So very, very real. That's what all my Confessions have shown me. I didn't live like I believed that, but now I try to live like I believe it Holy Confession is the greatest Sacrament. You have to trust the priest, and your sins have to be dealt with, and through the priest they are. Christ works through him.

I was born on July 22, the Feast of St. Mary Magdalene. My mother, who died on my 50th birthday, her baptismal name is Mary Magdelene Helen. I do not believe in coincidences. When I ask Jesus in Eucharistic Adoration what my name is, I hear "Sorrowful Joy." Because the sorrow for my sins was overwhelming. But God led me to receive the joy I received from my deep sorrow.

When I start writing in my notebook during Adoration, and don't look back until the hour is finished, when I go back and read, it's a surprise to me. I start out, "Dear Jesus," and I write Him a letter, and I write what comes to mind. Before I leave, I read what I wrote to Jesus, and I read what I felt He answered me in my heart, I know it's not me. I get so happy because I literally talked to Heaven and got an answer. I don't get an answer sometimes, and I see He doesn't want me to be asking about that. I sit there and wait. Confessing your sins is painful when you face yourself, to truly confess in honest openness to a priest. But afterward, the release that comes and the joy you receive are overwhelming. It doesn't happen in a one-time Confession. My journey began with one priest, but over the years I had Confessions with at least six of them.

Sketch by L.A. Spalding; used with permission.
"Mary," as envisioned by the artist, emerging from the depths of Hell.

In Adoration, God said to me that each of His sons He sent me had a special gift, and someone was praying for me all those years, when I was in and out of sin, when I was living a sinful life. It got to the point where the consequences of sin were coming at me, and then I turned to God. Then I would go back to my old ways.

It was like I was "dating" Him, off and on. I was so taken aback to learn this. He said I kept breaking up with Him. But He was always there, awaiting me. When I felt the consequences of my sinful life, when I turned to God, I was only giving Him lip service. My heart hadn't changed yet. But I went back to Him more and more, and then through priests in Confession I was given spiritual direction, and I realized so many things that I did offended God. I couldn't assume to go to God and still go back to the same way of life. Those weren't good Confessions.

It got to the point where I hit rock bottom. There was no other way to go but up. He put in my heart that the courtship was over. The dating was done. And now it was time for the marriage.

Every time I went to a different priest, each one brought forth another cleansing of a different part of my life. Then I worked on that part of my life. I didn't go looking for these priests. I went on different retreats and discovered each one had a beautiful gift. Each priest connected me to a different part of my life that needed attention.

Once I had come full circle, I not only wanted to love God, but I fell in love with God. And that's where my conversion really took root. Now I am to a point where I love God so much that every day when I wake up, I get on my knees to thank Him. I can't tell you what a gift it is to have a deliverance and a conversion. When you're going along in life and taking and not giving, when you're shown the effects to a soul and what that does to the whole human race, it is overwhelming. I don't want to be a part of that anymore. When you fall in love, you want to do everything for that person, and you will sacrifice anything and everything.

After one Confession, I closed my eyes and all I could see was the brightest emerald green—the brightest I ever saw green in my life. The priest said, "That is Hope."

Roses & Thorns

When I was 8 years old, I had a mystical experience. I experienced a spiritual ecstasy. I used to go to church in the morning. I went to Catholic school every day in Bethlehem, Pa. I used to go an hour ahead of time. I wanted to be with Jesus. I knelt there and looked at a giant crucifix and just kept saying over and over: *Jesus, I love you and love you*. I told Him I wanted Him to marry me. I don't know what happened after that. I knew I was there. I heard noise around me. But I wasn't aware of anything but Him. I was 8 years old and I remember it like it was yesterday.

Now I am 58. And God took 50 horrendous years of life, bringing my 8 and 58 together. Now I'm having roses, when all those years were thorns. Every day is like having roses. Every day is a blessing, no matter what happens. I can't tell you enough how thankful I am.

When I was growing up, I was very naïve. I wanted to go into the convent after the eighth grade, but they wouldn't let me. The Missionary Servants of the Precious Blood said I had to experience high school first. I wanted to be a Carmelite, because my grandmother used to take me to a Carmelite cloister. I witnessed one of the young women taking her final vows.

But when I went into high school, my life changed. I got involved with people who were wild. I was a rowdy teenager who didn't respect anything or anyone.

At 21, I married a guy younger than me who my parents did not like, and I married against their wishes. It was a rebellion. We got married in the Church, but there was no Mass, just a ceremony and a blessing. The man I married was very deceiving. He had spent time in prison. In high school, he got into a fight of jealousy over another girl, and punched the boy, who fell to the gym floor, hit his head, and died. My future husband went to prison for involuntary manslaughter. I visited him in prison.

He got out fairly quickly on good behavior and we moved to Florida where he was accepted into college. There, he got involved in gunrunning and drug-running. I worked three jobs so I had no clue about anything. When I did find out, we moved back to Pennsylvania. I thought everything would be OK.

But one day I brought my mother home to our house, and when we walked in, there was 10 pounds of marijuana on the dining room table. My mother lost it. I asked her if I could come home. I was 24. I came home. He wanted a divorce; I didn't. I was brought up that when you marry, you marry for life, and I thought somehow we could make it work. But he filed for divorce. I didn't contest it. I asked a priest, a monsignor who later passed away, why with my novenas, the more I prayed the worse it got? I did not understand it. He said, "The prayers are being answered. You don't understand it yet, but he is not the man God chose for you. This is a man you chose against your parent's wishes. You will find the man God chose."

The annulment—which my father insisted on, even though I said I would not get married again—was awful. I had to go alone to the tribunal. It was me and three priests. I had to answer all their questions. I was horrified at the time. I did not know half the things they were asking me. They were very detailed questions about my private life, and I wondered why priests wanted to know these things. They contacted my husband and he was extremely crude to them. He said he never wanted children, although he told me he did. So he lied to me, to the priest who married us, and everyone else. This was in the 1970s. An annulment was granted. †

I never saw him again, until this day.

But even after that, my life changed, and I went down the wrong path. I was devastated that my prayers weren't answered. I started doing drugs and drinking. I practically lived out of my car, and I left the Church. I totally turned away from God. I got fired from most of my jobs because I didn't show up. I was very arrogant. I said no guy would ever hurt me again. But I met a guy whose roommate bought an engagement ring from me where I worked at a

---

† **Author's note:** What is commonly called an "annulment" is more precisely a Declaration of Nullity. The Church states, upon investigation, that a marriage has one or more elements that are invalidating, according to canon law. So it declares a marriage null and void, because of various invalidating causes, according to divine and ecclesiastical law.

jewelry store. We went out and talked and talked and I told him how men were no good, and he shared how he had been hurt in his life. We'd been married 25 years on Nov. 23, 2009.

My husband, also an Italian Catholic, was raised by his grandmother. His mother gave him up when he was two.

But we were still away from the Church and started living together. I got pregnant and we decided to get married. We both went to Confession to the monsignor at my parish. So we started out right, in some way. As soon as I participated in that Mass, at my wedding, I knew something was going to change. I didn't want my child to have the atmosphere I was living in. I wanted it to be like when I grew up, close to the Church.

When my oldest daughter was little, I started taking her to church, but my husband never came. When she started kindergarten, I went to him and said she can't be living one life at school, and at home live another life. He said, "That's your thing, and not mine." I prayed and prayed. One Christmas Eve, by that time I had had my second child, my husband was out. I did not know where he went. I was making dinner. He came home, and I was ready to let him have it, and he said, "Merry Christmas! I went to Confession." And at that point he hadn't gone to Confession in six years. I cried and cried. So we went to church, as a family. And we're still doing that.

Words Fitly Spoken

As the years went by, I met good people and holy priests on yearly retreats. I went to retreats near Philadelphia and in New Jersey. I'll never forget when I met Monsignor Joseph James. You had to sign up to go to Holy Confession and take a number, and I learned from my friends that he had a special gift: He could read souls, and he took as long as he needed to with people, and sometimes people were in there for hours. He wouldn't eat much, and you often could see him prostrate, praying in front of the Blessed Sacrament.

I was with him for nearly two hours, and I can't share what happened, but when I came out, I felt as light as a feather. When my confession was done, he said he had been asked by God the Father to be my spiritual director and that we could speak by phone from where he was at Mercy Retreat Centers in Lubbock, Texas. I couldn't believe it. I learned there were only 60 people in the United States who had spiritual direction with the Monsignor, and somehow, I was one of them.

That was the beginning. Sometimes what he told me got me mad: Who does this person think he is? He's not God. But every time he called me to prepare me for a family tragedy, it happened. I learned to trust the Lord, whatever happened.

Then he had a heart attack. He wrote me a letter one Christmas, and told me my spiritual direction had to stop. I said, "Father, I will never get into Heaven without you!" He said, "Yes, you will. There are many good priests." I told him, "Father, I need your prayers; I will pray for you."

But even after that, I learned through great priests that I needed to improve the quality of my confessions, and after one particularly difficult encounter at a retreat, I fell on my bed in my room. I cried so hard to the Lord, that I literally heard a voice telling me to go to a page in the Bible, the Catholic Revised Standard Version: Page 435. It ended up being Proverbs 25. The whole proverb was a rude awakening to me: "It is the glory of God to conceal things, but the glory of kings is to search things out A word fitly spoken is like apples of gold in a setting of silver."

I had been thinking I was a good Catholic, and was holy. But you can't think like that. One sin has so many years of Purgatory on it. If you keep doing it over and over, you never get out of it. I learned in Adoration that Jesus came to me when I was a child at 8 years old, and now he was coming back to me at 58, and he wanted to wipe those 50 years away as if all the horror of sin was gone. I could see: *This time I was not turning back.*

In 2008, I decided to do a "life review" Confession. I saw my confessor on Ash Wednesday, and made my best Confession ever. I wrote down my sins, for all 50 years, the slightest thing to the greatest thing. I'd hide my list between my mattress and my box spring so my family didn't see it. I went through the commandments, all the virtues, and the seven capital sins in detail. It is important to make it as clear to the priest as possible so you get the proper penance. If you downplay a mortal sin because you are embarrassed and make it sound like it's a venial sin, the priest gives a penance for a venial sin. When you make an unworthy Confession, you don't receive the sacramental absolution efficaciously. In fact, it's a sinful and sacrilegious Confession.

No one knows what a sin is anymore. People do not know how to confess.

When I left after that Holy Confession, I couldn't tell what cloud I was on. I sang all the way home. It was the first time I felt this. I literally came in contact with Heaven 101. I thanked God for all the priests who led me there. I will pray for them, today and every day. I literally gave my whole life back to God. He literally gave me a whole new start. It's like you come right out of the womb.

My life is so different. I am still weak. I still sin. But when I go to Confession, it's different now. I say my sins differently. I am 58 years old and I finally know how to go to Confession.

Heaven is filled with great sinners who became great saints and I am going to get in! I don't have to be popular or well-known. I owe it all to a good priest, a priest who isn't afraid to tell it like it is. We need more priests like that because it's the priest who represents Christ who brings you through. I have relatives who won't go to their parish priest because he knows them. They go out of their way to go to another priest. You're confessing to Christ! He's going to know you anyway. I never understood that. It's good to have a priest who knows you. He can help you better.

Mercy Bestowed, Mercy Given

I'm on fire now. I'll help anyone who comes to me. I thank God, every time I go into a church. I say, "I am so sorry I strayed. Thank you for bringing me back." I could have been dead so many times. I could have been killed with the people I hung around with. God saved me and brought me back.

When I go to Adoration each Friday, I review the whole week since the last time I sat in front of the Blessed Sacrament. I sit with pen and paper and place myself in

God's presence and give Him praise. I thank Him for this time one-on-one. I tell Him what I did that offended Him and what I did that pleased Him. Many times I sit there and I just wait. What He'll always show is where I offend Him first. Then He'll always be very gentle and tell me small steps I can take. Jesus always tells me small steps.

Then I ask if there was anything at all that I did that pleased Him. I am more interested in where I don't please Him so that I can please Him more. I come out of Adoration feeling so hopeful. I am working on humility. It's very hard. I was a very prideful person. He's showing me pride is involved in everything.

I had a wonderful journey with these priests, and every Thursday I offer my day for the souls of all priests, especially those who have impacted my life. I pray for all the priests in Purgatory. I pray for all priests who have lost their desire to say the Mass reverently. I pray for priests who misguide people in Confession. I pray for priests who don't believe in the True Presence in the Eucharist anymore. We need to pray for priests. They are really attacked.

I'm glad God has given me this time to repent. God showed me to watch how I talk to people, and how to use my voice, the words I say. I was an opinionated, aggressive person all my life, and now I am trying to use my gifts in a godly way, not a condescending way. I am much more aware of my actions, extremely aware. God gave me an illumination in these confessions, things I took for granted. You think you're doing so well, but when you get a good authentic examination of conscience, that's what makes a difference. I'm taking care of my elderly father now. He will be 85 this year. My parents separated when I was a kid. My father abused my mother. She forgave him and took him back.

They were married 53 years before she died. I take care of him now, but I hated him back then with a passion. I would sleep with a crucifix under my pillow while I listened to him hurt her. When my mother said, after they separated, "Your father is coming home," I said, "How could you take him back?" And she said, "I'll tell you right now, young lady, when you get married, everyone is entitled to a second chance. You must forgive."

The greatest gift my mother ever gave me was to teach me that. Here he is now, a little old man. He used to be a giant of a man, and now I am taking care of him.

It's funny how God reminds us, in the length of our lives, our everyday lives, all that He has done for us, to save us, to bring us home to Him. When we see it, living a life of atonement is a blessing, a beautiful, beautiful blessing.~ ☧

✝

Daily Examination of Conscience

Thanksgiving. I thank the Lord with all my heart for the gifts I've received from God this day.

Self Awareness. I ask God for the grace to know how I've accepted these gifts or how I've refused to use them.

Examination. Aware of God's loving presence, I examine my thoughts, my words, my actions of the day, paying special attention to my underlying feelings. Above all, I seek to know how God has been at work in my life, drawing me to the Divine in events of the day. I seek to know if sins or faults have drawn me away from God, or placed obstacles between us.

Forgiveness. I thank God from my heart for the ways I've been drawn to Him. I beg God's pardon and forgiveness for my sins—for allowing myself to be drawn away.

Renewal. I thank the Lord for His goodness and mercy, which I received this day. I beg for a new and generous heart as I follow Him in the coming day.

Prayer. I say the Our Father.

Prayer to Reconcile with Christ after Grave Sin

Lord, Jesus Christ, only Son of the Father, through your Passion and Death on the Cross you have purchased for us the glory of everlasting life. Through your Most Precious Blood and Sacred Body, grant me perfect contrition in confessing my sins, to do penance and reparation, and to atone for them. May I diligently, through your bounteous grace, avoid all occasion and near occasion of sin. *Through Jesus Christ, Our Lord,* **Amen.**

"Everything seems to me to pass so quickly that we must concentrate on how to die rather than on how to live. How sweet it is to die if one has lived on the Cross with Christ."
~ **St. Teresa of Avila**

Love for Life

Chapter 4

Saint John Mary Vianney said *even the angels* are overwhelmed by the mystery of the priesthood.

As far superior as the angels are to us, they don't have this mediation power—man working through Christ in the priesthood. St. Francis of Assisi is said to have observed: *"If I saw an angel and a priest, I would bend my knee first to the priest and then to the angel."* St. Peter Damien said all the angels in Heaven cannot absolve from a single sin. Even our Blessed Virgin Mother bows before a priest, for he is Christ! And listen to St. Bernadine of Siena: *"Holy Virgin, excuse me, for I speak not against thee: the Lord has raised the priesthood above thee."* The Blessed Virgin bore the Savior once to the world. A priest does so at every Mass.

We cannot understand the exquisite splendor of ordination's power. St. Vianney, one of the holiest of priests, marveled: "The priest will only be understood in Heaven. If we were to understand him on this Earth, we would die of love."

Can you imagine? *Dying of love?* Only in heaven will we begin to appreciate and thank God for the priestly vocation. When people understand—as St. Vianney did—that the priesthood is the love of the heart of Jesus, seminaries will fill again. Young people will be on fire, lining up at the confessional, beating down their church's doors, just to get their pastor's blessing.

The mystics have said St. Joseph, patron of the Universal Church, died of love in the arms of Jesus and our Blessed Mother, literally surrounded with love. After all, God is love. Before the existence of any created thing, God loved. St. John tells us this in his first letter *(1 John 4:8)*.

So a priest's mission isn't his own. It's Christ's mission, united in Triune Love. We'll never fully comprehend Divine Love, but we can compare it to fatherly love, a Josephite love, motherly love, a Marian love, the priestly love I try to convey on these pages. The true love Christ gives us through the priest is most apparent in the Holy Eucharist, the source and summit of all Sacraments.

But we need to be reminded of this Love, this route to true life, over and over, for we're human, tarnished by original sin and by new mortal and venial sins. We need to be brought to this Love, to touch it, to let it fill us, to transform our suffering, to allow us to look at everything in the novel way Christ promised, *"Behold, I make all things new" (Rev 21:5)*. Do this and we fully realize its saving and healing power—but only if we allow our hearts to be opened by the supernatural grace we receive through Holy Hands.

I see the realization of this love in the ministry, with which, by the grace of God, I've been blessed. I see it when people recognize fully that all life is sacred, because our souls are formed in love. Life is so sacred that God appoints to each of us a guardian angel (*Catechism of the Catholic*

Church, 352) to guide us, yet who simultaneously beholds Him in the Beatific Vision. St. Jerome said, "How great the dignity of the soul, since each one has from his birth an angel commissioned to guard it" *(Comm. in Matt., xviii, lib. II).* But like the supernatural reality of the priesthood, this transcendent reality, too, has been lost through the years.

I recall the mother of a pregnant teenage girl who told me friends and doctors were pressuring the girl to abort the child. Only it wasn't one baby. Or two. The young girl was expecting triplets.

And the doctors said, "She's only 18. She should terminate the pregnancy. Her life's in danger." The girl, a Catholic who already knew the sanctity of life, was distraught, and her mother said, "I know she won't get an abortion, but she's emotionally fragile. Everyone's putting pressure on her, even her so-called friends."

She asked me to talk to the girl. I told the young mother-to-be: "God not only blessed you, but guess what? He blessed you with three guardian angels. You have three unborn children, so you have their three guardian angels and your own." She smiled. "So you have four angels here. There are eight of you here now. These angels are so happy for these babies. Let's pray with them. They don't want the babies killed."

We prayed, and she started talking again: "These babies are from God. God wants them to live. I want them to live. Even if I have to die, I want these babies to have a chance to be baptized so they too can go to heaven." Beautiful. Imagine someone saying, "I want the babies to live even if the babies live only for a moment to be baptized." She was willing to risk her own life to give her babies a chance at eternal life, to atone for her lack of chastity.

By the grace of God, the girl gave birth to three girls. What a testimony to love. To life! What courage. What virtue in her realizing the importance of purity as a young adult. But how did she arrive at that place? By grace, a realization of what was at stake, supernaturally, through brief prayer and conversation with a priest, someone who helped open her eyes, and her soul, to all that is seen and unseen.

A Child's Eternal Gift

Yet even that beautiful affirmation of life is only a preamble to the overwhelming supernatural merit of the stories I'm about to share through the words of two other loving mothers. These stories are so multidimensional, to two families and to my ministry, that they defy full understanding, even upon reflection. Reflect on them. See how the stories live in communion, but happened nearly without these mothers being aware of each other's lives or their losses. Yet, where suffering exists, grace abounds. Look to the Cross! Look deep within the mystical Body of Christ.

Consider the dying child, beautiful Mairead. She was born on Jan. 22, 2003, the 30th anniversary of *Roe vs. Wade,* a legal decision that opened the door to allow the abortion of more than 50 million American children. This child lived a brief life of suffering. Yet, by the logic of her culture, she shouldn't have been born at all.

But Mairead's life is a spiritual banquet. Her suffering tests her family and then renews their Catholic faith, and their devotion to the family Rosary. Her pain and trials bring healing to untold others who put aside their own anguish to pray for her at an evening healing service.

Mairead's family undergoes a crisis of faith. For no one thought this tiny, beautiful child should be allowed to suffer as she did, her head bandaged, her soft moaning heard throughout the church the night of the service. But somehow, the night became peaceful, serene. I felt God touch Mairead and her family. After I exposed the Blessed Sacrament for Adoration during the service, when I saw Mairead, I heard the Lord in my heart: *Take me to her.*

I turned, and as I picked up the monstrance with the Blessed Sacrament, hundreds of people spontaneously fell to their knees. They went silent. I could feel the intensity of people praying. Even though they had cancers and illnesses and all sorts of personal afflictions—everyone was attuned to this tiny child. And after the family came up for a blessing, I told everyone they were offering their sufferings for this baby. And the baby brought healing and conversion to these prayerful people of faith.

I never felt such complete, united, spontaneous prayer for a single intention in my entire ministry. It was profound. There was a healing, real power. Christ allowed me to bring the Holy Eucharist to her—*His heart burning with compassion* —so that He could give her a year more of life, so that her family could grow beyond their test, and say goodbye.

There were changes in the tumor that was supposed to have killed Mairead that couldn't be explained. In fact, there was a significant change just weeks after the healing service, with a biopsy confirming that parts of the tumor were dead, *necrotic* in medical terminology—that couldn't be explained.

Doctors said normally no changes are seen until six months after chemotherapy. Yet this was before chemotherapy, and four weeks after Mairead was blessed. But God, in His Infinite Mercy, takes it *beyond* Mairead. The oblation of Mairead's brief life still transforms and sustains my ministry! In that moment, when I was moved to do something spontaneous for the Lord to attend to His poor suffering little one, I felt a spiritual energy, the spiritual fraternity of the priesthood, being solicitous and crying out toward *my* spiritual daughter.

In my priesthood, I felt the power of her intercession, her suffering, and I still feel it even now that she's in Heaven. After all, as a priest, I am a spiritual father, a shepherd to all. But Our Lord gave me my own special connection with Mairead.

I feel that when I am ministering to all people. I minister to babies who are baptized, unborn babies in the womb, right through to the elderly and infirm. But that moment was a poignant encounter, and I was aware that it developed grace in my fatherhood as a priest. I was blessed with a gift that did not come from me, but in giving the gift, it transformed me, and the ministry given to me by God.

This baby's life, her vocation, and even her condition, brought people to holiness. She sanctified her caregivers, and they could see what a gift Mairead was. *What a gift, her life!* Even now, since we have her as our intercessor in Heaven. Mairead is able to work miracles, still, through my ministry. Most people would be overwhelmed to even think that; they don't understand things like that. Now that she is in the glory of Eternity, her baptismal innocence maintained, she experiences the power of the Resurrection. She and others

like her are awaiting the resurrection of their bodies, awaiting the Last Judgment. But they're powerful intercessors.
They're in the Communion of Saints. Her guardian angel,
too. I invoke Mairead's angel often for prayers.

Mairead's story doesn't end with her family or my
ministry, however. After all, the superabundant graces of
our Savior, even if from the fringe of His garment, touched
everyone in the church that night. Supernatural grace caused
one woman to come forward, to share her story. I call her
Elise. I've changed her children's names, too, to protect her
privacy, and their dignity.

At the same healing service in which beautiful Mairead
is given months more to live through an encounter with
Christ in the Holy Eucharist, Elise, unknown to the girl's
family, begins healing from a past that includes an alcoholic
father, two of three children out of wedlock, and a tragic
loss. Elise was drawn to the service because one of her
children, an autistic boy, was healed of night terrors and
improved in his condition after I blessed his photo, brought
to me by Elise's neighbor, Maria.

At the healing service, which begins the transformation
of this penitent mother's life, she recognizes Mairead's
suffering, a suffering far beyond hers for her son, and she
feels compelled to give a special gift to Mary, Mairead's
mother. But I'll let these women share their stories,
and those of their two children, Michael and Mairead, a
boy and a girl born five months apart. Read and absorb
their testimonies. Shepherded toward Christ, these mothers
and their families now share a growing realization of
gifts that come to hearts open to the possibility of
Divine Love, through hands He's chosen to be His own.

Photo courtesy of the Feeney family.
Mairead Feeney, at 1 year old, now a child of God.

Mary Begins Mairead's Story

Mary   She weighed seven pounds. I worried because her delivery was induced, and lasted a long time. My husband, Sean, and I were at the hospital all night. But she seemed healthy and strong. Then, in a few weeks, she tended to gag on her baby formula. Her right eye jiggled back and forth.

At her four-month checkup, the doctor called it *nystagmus,* an involuntary eye movement, and sent us to an ophthalmologist. She was very fussy and didn't want to eat.

Between the four- and six-month checkups, she gained only an ounce.

For all of us, even later, when we said she was going through so much, she was still smiling. She had this smile. Even when things got bad, it told us: *We can still be strong.*

After her six-month checkup, things got scary. She started to run a fever, and they did X-rays and blood work. Her white count was low and she had *bronchiolitis*. It was summer, so it was strange.

We canceled the ophthalmologist appointment when my father-in-law, Sean's dad, Jack, passed away. I think at that point, our faith was being tested. It was very hard dealing with his loss. He and Sean's mom, Mary, were married 50 years.

Why did this happen, we asked, right when we lost Sean's dad? We had a close family and we went to church. Why was this happening to us?

And yet as we struggled, both our families were there for us. My mom and dad, Kathleen and Pat O'Grady, later would stay in the hospital. They also cared for my other three small children. All Sean's sisters and my two sisters and two brothers helped us. A week later, Mairead's other eye started wiggling. The eye doctor said it seemed to be caused by something pressuring her brain. They wanted to do an MRI.

The night before our appointment with a pediatric specialist, I said to Sean—at 3 o'clock in the morning— "I think it's a brain tumor." A CT scan showed a tumor the size of a small fist in her brain. That was causing the pressure on her eyes, causing them to wiggle, and on the hypothalamus, which controls appetite. She needed surgery to relieve the pressure. As soon as they had a diagnosis, they admitted her to the hospital.

As we waited for the surgeon, I thought Mairead was dying. She went limp. They rushed her in for surgery. They said if they had not operated in time, she would have died from the pressure in her brain.

Elise Worries About Michael

Elise   I thought my son hated me. He did nothing but cry and scream, and wouldn't cuddle. I thought God was punishing me for having him out of wedlock. He'd get night terrors. He'd run through the house with his eyes open, but he'd be asleep. His dreams were very scary.

I was getting no sleep, and working all the time. I had to move to Section 8 housing, because I couldn't afford anything else. I needed help. I didn't know anyone, and I was sinking deeper into hopelessness and depression. I paid the bills according to what we needed. I picked up second shift bartending, and I was working from 10 a.m. to 3 a.m. the next day. I got used to not sleeping and Michael wouldn't sleep anyway. I had a babysitter who'd watch Michael and my daughter, Rose—this was before I had my littlest, James—until 3 a.m. Then I'd wake them up after work to take them home.

Michael kept getting worse. He'd get violent attacks. Something would trigger him and he'd throw something. He would go into convulsions whenever he ate. The babysitter was having a hard time with him. I had to quit my job. I had $182 a month to feed three of us. Maybe I hurt people, I thought, but I don't think I deserve this. I hit a point when I prayed to God for my kids to have a better upbringing.

Then I met Maria, this beautiful Croatian woman, and something clicked with her. She saw I was in complete desperation. Maria explained God does not come after you; He loves you, but that the devil attacks you. She took Michael's picture to one of your healing services, Father, and after that, the night terrors stopped.

I called Maria whenever I felt like I couldn't handle anything. Maria taught me to pray the Rosary. She explained how you have to pray for your enemies. She was someone I looked forward to seeing every day. She was the only light in my darkness. I saw the light because of Maria and the prayers.

Things started looking up. I got a job as a dental assistant, and my son was diagnosed when he was two years old. He was at a 5-month-old's level. The tears came when they told me he had an illness on the autism spectrum. I was dumbfounded. But I found another blessing, Linda, a babysitter who could handle him, but then she couldn't help, and had to focus on her own four children.

It was at that point that everything spiraled out of control. I was trying very hard to understand. But I had Maria praying for me and telling me: "Say the Rosary." I was saying the Rosary on my First Communion beads, which were pink glass beads. For some reason, I kept seeing rainbows everywhere.

One day at work an old man grabbed my hand. He was 92 years old and his name was Ben, and he said, "You can't take care of your children, unless you take care of yourself." It was a message for my whole life: I had never taken care of *me*. I told Dr. Angie, my boss at the dental office, and she said, "God's talking to you."

Maria told me that you, Father, were coming here, and she arranged for me to see you at the healing service. Before I went, she told me to grab my Rosary and say my prayers. I did, and the next day its links turned from silver to gold. I looked down and couldn't believe it. I had had these since second grade. Maria lived nearby and I ran downstairs and knocked on her door: "Look at my Rosary beads!"

She said, "When did that happen?"

I said, "Last night."

She showed me her beads, and they were all golden. She said, "The Blessed Mother is calling you to her Son." I looked at her and I was so thankful I was going to the healing Mass. I looked at the Rosary beads and thought, *Something here is different. I have to pay attention to these signs.*

Mairead Receives a Blessing

Mary   After they put a shunt in to drain the fluid in Mairead's head, they bandaged her head. They gave her medications to increase her appetite. We had her home a short time before she would start chemotherapy. We set up an oncologist appointment.

The healing Mass was at St. Bridget's, on Saturday Aug. 23, 2003.

Sean and I both went to Catholic schools, so we have a strong faith. Religion is a part of our life. We always tried to live by God's rules as best we can as Christians. Our parents were always very religious. Sean's mom goes to Mass every day. Many of our family members carry their Rosary beads. We've always had our Rosaries by the bedside, but I can't say prior to that that I said the Rosary all the time. So I don't think I ever gave 100 percent of my faith and belief to God. I knew I needed to pray more, to have my family more involved in our faith.

I knew Poppy, Sean's dad, Jack, and Uncle Joe, my sister-in-law's husband, were watching over Mairead from Heaven. My sister-in-law, Karen, has a strong faith, and felt that Joe, whom she lost when he was 41, was indeed watching over us. I knew if anything terrible happened, Poppy and Uncle Joe and other family members would take care of Mairead in Heaven.

It wasn't like we didn't have faith, but we questioned it, with Mairead and with my brother-in-law, Joe, who we saw suffer and die from lung cancer that spread to his brain. We saw how debilitating it was. When we heard it was Mairead's brain, it was a real test for us, especially since we had lost Jack four weeks prior. It was hard.

I never had been to a healing Mass, or rather, a healing service after the Mass. I never knew they had healing services. When I found out from someone at our church, Our Lady of Knock Shrine, I was so happy. Mairead was home from the hospital. The family was up to see her. They were able to come with us, and that meant a lot. I don't think anyone had been to a healing Mass so I didn't know what to expect. It was a very beautiful and touching Mass. For some reason, I remember Mairead looking up at the light in the church.

I remember you blessing her, Father. You stood there a long time, longer than you were with other people receiving a blessing, and you were praying and praying. It was very intense on Mairead. You were so focused on her. My goodness, I've never been prayed over like that! I remember getting a strange feeling. You left us and came back with the Blessed Sacrament and held it over her for the longest time.

As we left, I realized, "My God, he didn't do that for anybody else. Why her?" I do remember you asking me her name, and I said, "It's Mairead, a Gaelic name for Margaret." And you said, "I love the name Mairead." I was shocked you knew how to say it. There was something special about that. I remember thinking that maybe somehow you could help us. All of us felt like that.

Four weeks after the healing service with you, Father, the doctors did the biopsy. It was Sept. 24. The night before, I thought it may be our last Sunday dinner with her. But she got through the biopsy.

The biopsy confirmed that the tumor's gray areas had been living tissue, but now they were dead, *necrotic*. That was when the doctor said they normally don't see changes until six months after the start of chemotherapy. I wrote this in my journal—maybe, you, Fr. Machado, had done something! I truly believed it was partly due to your prayers, since it was only four weeks after the healing service. Our initial thought was, "The blessing caused some of the tumors to die."

And as I look back on it now, it's strange to me that the day I learned that parts of the tumor were dead, it was a year from that day, Oct. 9, that Mairead died. I wrote an exclamation point in my journal when I realized this. The doctors said they had never seen parts of the tumor dead so quickly. So it was no question that you, Father, had done something to cause this.

After the biopsy, I noticed her right side wasn't moving. A scan showed she had had a stroke. She started having seizures. The doctor told us since she had one stroke, the possibility of another was high.

The *glioma* was the treatable type. And the doctors thought with chemotherapy, there was great hope.

Even with the complications, they thought it was going to work. We hoped she could beat this, because it looked like the tumor started to die. But even though there were dead parts, it continued to change.

They told us the strokes could turn her into a "vegetable." We had to decide whether to sign "do not resuscitate" forms. We didn't sign them; we couldn't make that decision. How intense it was, and they thought she could be gone, again. Here we thought we lost her the first day when she was diagnosed, and once again we thought she would not make it through the night. And she got through.

They regulated the seizures. The swelling decreased. But we didn't know what to do. It was a horrible thing. I didn't want her to die and I did not want to keep her alive if her brain was dead.

We got though that night and the next morning. She was very bad. My sister Geraldine was there at 4:30 a.m. Sean's family was there.

We were joined by everyone because it was such a terrible night. There was a priest there, Fr. Bob, who told us it was the Feast of the Archangels, Sept. 29. Mairead started to look better. My husband asked his sister Debbie to lead a Rosary in the hospital room. We had never done that as a large group before. We prayed and prayed. And she sat up in the bed that next day. She lay in bed with me. I got her dressed. That night she was better. They didn't know how she had gotten through. They gave her seizure medications. From that point she did get a little better.

On Erin's first day of kindergarten, Mairead got her first tooth, and it was her first day of chemotherapy. But her body had an allergic reaction to the chemotherapy. By the time the new scans came in December, because she was not on the appropriate chemo, they revealed the tumor was growing again. The doctors recommended taking out the tumor, or most of it.

Sean's sister Mary Jeanne, who is a nurse, helped us through all the doctor's appointments, explaining everything. A specialist in Boston asked: "Have you seen the scans? Take her home and let her die peacefully." The doctor said the tumor was so large that "debulking" the tumor could be dangerous.

Our doctor recommended a specialist, the top surgeon in the country.

The idea was that if she could live a few more years, she had a higher chance of survival, since in younger children, *gliomas* grow more quickly. The doctor said chemotherapy worked for this tumor and with continuous chemotherapy, hopefully it would shrink. She tried so many different types of chemotherapy, yet the tumor still grew.

So we made the decision to do the debulking, with the top surgeon in the country. There was a chance of her being blind after so many complications, but that she could survive. So that was our "choice," we had to make a decision. Although she originally was scheduled for surgery March

18, she had so many complications—fevers, infections, issues with her shunt, and 36 days of hospitalization—that she didn't get the surgery until May. It was very difficult.

The debulking surgery on May 6 lasted nearly 10 hours and when the surgeon came out; he said they debulked 75 percent of the tumor.

It was there, in that hospital, that she lost her smile, and she just kind of laid there with a blank stare. She lost everything. She didn't respond to much at all.

She came home May 14. She was still shaking, and being tested for seizures. She couldn't move. She continued to have many complications, and the tumor spread to her spine.

Mairead Gifts Elise; Elise Responds

I had an abortion, after my first son. At that point I was a murderer. I wanted to die myself. I had no family around me. My friends disappeared. I had no phone, no television, not enough money to eat. I felt I didn't deserve to live. So at the healing service, when I looked at this baby, Mairead, it shook me.

I'm complaining about sleeping, about having a child I don't know because of his condition. But I decided at that Mass to get my son baptized. Even though I felt like neither of us belonged in church—all he did was scream and run around and people gave me dirty looks—I decided to do it. I remember looking at baby Mairead and I couldn't stop crying. The tears just kept coming and coming. I was thinking about her and her family, and here I killed a child, and here's a child that's suffering for other people. I was so full of shame. What a beautiful angel this child was. And when she winced in pain, it was like someone took a dagger to my heart.

I remember crying hysterically through the whole Mass, and hearing a baby crying. What I experienced during Mass I find hard to describe. I would look at Mairead, she would cry out in pain every two minutes, and I'd think, "Here I have a boy out of control—dear God, I am lucky!"

Dr. Angie, Maria, and my aunt, Carol, were there. When I looked at the altar, I saw a white light. Not thick, but a real bright light, Father. Rays of bright light surrounded you. I said, "Oh my, there is something really special about this," and I looked around for anyone else's reaction.

I kept hearing a baby cry. I was distracted. I said, "Dear God, I don't belong here, I am asking for help with my son." Because of my son I could never go to church. I was missing Mass for a year or two. But something different was going on here, at this Mass.

Father, when you raised the Host, I could see you almost talking to someone. When you raised the Host, it was like—*PHOOOF!*—flames of pure white, the brightest white, up to the ceiling. I was shocked. No one else had a reaction. I tapped my aunt: "Do you see the white light?" "No," she said, but she smiled. I asked Dr. Angie, "Do you see white light?" Maria answered for her, "No, but I have heard of that happening."

It was during the Consecration, but I know you're not supposed to talk, but it was amazing. When you had finished consecrating the Precious Blood, it slowly died down. White flames? I rubbed my eyes. This is crazy. When it came time for my blessing, I went up and brought Michael's picture, and you prayed over the picture and me. But I still did not surrender, to Jesus.

I didn't understand even though I made my First Communion and was a Catholic forever, that I did not have a relationship with the Eucharist or Jesus. I wouldn't know how powerful that could be. But the idea of going to a healing Mass was new to me, and I was trying to make sense of what I saw. I felt like I was losing my mind. And seeing the baby, it ripped my heart out. "I don't deserve to be here," I thought.

People were lined up talking to Mairead's family after the healing service. I walked up to her mother and she smiled. I was speechless. Somehow I got out some words: "Here, these are my First Communion Rosary beads. I feel compelled to give them to you. They're special and she's special." I barely felt worthy to speak to her. It's like all your sins come out through your pores when you look at someone like that. Who am I to talk to these people? It was very humbling. Afterward, I missed those beads. They were my miracle beads.

Mary Prays for Pink Roses

I do remember speaking with a lady, and I know she gave me her Rosary beads.

We spoke afterward, and I know she was there for a reason. She said she was putting her prayers in for Mairead, instead of the things she was praying for. All of my brothers and my sister and Sean's sisters and parents were moved and touched by the experience of the healing service. Prior to that, we didn't always say the Rosary. I started. Sean is saying it more.

After the debulking surgery, Mairead would sit in her rocking seat, not moving. They determined she was blind. The cancer began affecting her body and she couldn't walk. She couldn't see. She couldn't do anything. Before, she used to sit on her own. She used to say "momma" and blow kisses, even after the biopsy. She'd put her little finger in her mouth because she was teething.

I prayed to St. Thérèse of Lisieux. The pink rose was my sign. Every time I asked for a sign and prayed, I would see a rose. It would give me strength. It would give me chills when I'd see one. I know someone in Heaven was looking over us and giving us strength.

Karen told me she prayed to St. Thérèse. I always loved St. Thérèse, I knew she was a young girl when she passed away, and she always gave the sign of her little rose. My confirmation name is Thérèse. I did a report on her. I always felt I had someone to pray to. With Mairead, I did become more willing to pray to St. Thérèse. I knew she would understand because she was ill so much as a child. It seemed to me whenever I prayed to her, if I asked for a sign, somehow a sign was given.

One time I was thinking, which sign would she give so I would know she was listening, and there was an artist on a PBS channel teaching how to draw a rose—"Oh my gosh, there you go! A sign!"

A friend, a lady Eucharistic Minister who moved away, but who prayed for Mairead, she worked for a pro-life clinic, an organization to help save people, to prevent abortions. Once she sent me a little pink rose, a rose and a little angel,

I thought maybe St. Thérèse was working through her to get to me.

Michael Gets Baptized

I had my son baptized a week or two after the healing Mass. Because he never stopped moving, I couldn't get him baptized, I couldn't keep him in the church. Maria would bring me bulletins so that I could read the Sunday gospel. My mother warned the pastor before the baptism that Michael would be a little difficult. Michael was more out of control than normal, however, screaming. He tried shaking the baptismal font. He was growling and yelling and running. He was acting like a demon, that's what he looked like. I saw Maria in deep prayer.

I felt like a horrible mom. People in the back had their mouths open.

Maria said, "That's good. These people need to see what you're dealing with."

I was looking at Michael: "Please be good." It took two of us to hold him down while the priest poured water on him. He was screaming and wriggling. But as soon as we put his white stole on him, he was calm. I looked at my mother, and my mother's mouth was open. I had a different child. He wasn't screaming and having fits every two seconds. I could eat a meal. It was wonderful. It was amazing. The next day he reverted to the way he was. But I wondered how many more signs I'd be getting. I still didn't get it.

Michael's therapies were going well. I also was receiving counseling. In the evening, Maria was there. A downstairs neighbor prayed with us. She told me to look into proper nutrition for Michael, and it was almost like doors started opening. I started seeing tiny improvements in him from all his therapies. I was reading medical journals. And I was reading "God Calling," a devotional book that has a different message every day, which Maria gave me. I was reading more and more about my faith and understanding more and finding joy in what I was doing. The more I found out about autism, the more I thought, "I am going to help heal him no matter what it takes."

His first word was *"Wow!"* All of sudden, he was opening up more and more, with sign language. I begged the county early intervention office for a nutritionist and I was researching diet and the effects of diet. My mom bought vitamins, and fruits and vegetables, integrating them into his meals. I would not give him cookies, which he loved, until he signed, "I want a cookie."

It took eight months before he ate more and before he had an adverse reaction—going into convulsions even— to some foods. He would run screaming and break something. When he came around a corner in the house and said "I want a cookie," motioning with his hand, I got on the ground and I was in tears, "Oh my God, yes! You can have three cookies!" He was communicating for the first time! And I thought, "He's coming back to me!"

All the time I was thanking and praising God. It's amazing, he's showing such progress. He still has a long way to go. But I started thinking, "I can do this. I can definitely do this."

Mairead Dies in Her Mother's Arms

We got to the point of how much more can this little girl go through? I remember going to the doctor, and he said, "Probably you have a week." The weight of the tumor suppressed everything. Her breathing was off. I remember coming home, praying: *"God, is there something else we can do?"* At the very end, she was in the hospital for another infection, and I wanted her at home. I thought there was no reason for me to sit in the hospital when I have three other kids at home. We brought her home, and had hospice care. The doctor told us to look for the signs, such as rapid breathing. That morning I knew. I called my mom and said, "Come."

I called our families to come, and many of them were here. And Mairead's breathing was just off. It was 6 p.m.

She passed in my arms on the couch.

I held her for hours, I didn't move. I just sat on the couch and held her and held her and held her. In the morning, I felt her going to Heaven. I heard her saying, *"Mom, I'm free! I'm free! I'm free!"*

It was fall, and I could see the fall leaves. I envisioned her flying through them to the mountains, and I was smiling. How could I be smiling? My daughter just died. But there was freedom. She was finally free.

It was 22 months she survived. I remember thinking: She had 17 surgeries in 14 months. It was an outrageous number. More than how many months old she was at the time. Two days after when we had the wake, Karen, my sister-in-law, had a stroke. We were *really* tested. She is the one I got a lot of strength from, and it was her husband who died of cancer at 41. Every day at the hospital, she was there. She is doing better now; she loved Mairead.

After a terrible tragedy, you get discouraged, then you regain it all, because you get to thinking about what happened and why. I have a stronger faith now, and I know she is with God in Heaven. I do feel like I should be doing more. Praying more. I have started teaching religion class to my daughter Erin's fifth-grade class, and the sixth-grade class.

Anyone who has heard of Mairead sent us cards. Hundreds and hundreds of people sent Mass cards, letters of inspiration. Friends of our families in a tight-knit Irish community in two parishes—one here and in New York City—who we knew but not always well, organized a benefit to offset the cost of her surgeries and complications when she was still struggling—1,000 people came. It showed us what people do in times of crisis. People I hardly knew, who remembered me from when I was a baby, or were friends of my father, they donated money, they gave us anything and everything.

After Mairead passed, we had two more boys, Brendan, and Kevin, which are a gift from her as well. So we have five children. When she passed away, we had a lot of pink roses, at the gravesite. It was comforting to me to know that St. Thérèse was listening and helping us and watching over us.

Mairead is always with me. It's Mairead who has given us the strength. And God, well, I wonder why He wanted her. She has touched people, and everywhere we go people tell us, "I still pray to Mairead." I still talk to Mairead. But people I would not expect to tell me that. I think of her all the time. I don't want people forgetting her. I have aunts, and they say she is always in their prayers. They are always asking for her help with this and that. She has touched so many lives that we don't even know. She did something for them. Maybe sharing her story is a way of being able to say *thank you*.

Elise Begins to See

Sometimes we are supposed to suffer because it's a redemptive thing. If you don't suffer, you can't evolve into what God wants you to be. I finally realize now how hard it is to embrace suffering when it happens. When I went through all this with my son, I suffered every day of my life. If I didn't, I wouldn't be in the place where I am now.

I am really thankful. ~ΑΩ

✝

Prayer for Healing from the Loss of a Child

Almighty and Everlasting God, as you've called this baptized child into the glory of your Son's Kingdom, and embraced him (her) with your paternal love, where he (she) goes may we hope to follow, at the end of our earthly pilgrimage.

Dearest baptized child, as you are a Saint in Heaven, now intercede and pray for us, that we may find hope, consolation, and sanctification here below and one day share in the Beatific Vision in the Life to come. *Through Jesus Christ, Our Lord,* **Amen.**

Prayer for Healing from an Abortion [†]

Oh gracious and merciful Lord, grant me the contrition to recognize that I have murdered my unborn baby, that I am overwhelmed with grief, and that I may repent in reparation for the most egregious sin of abortion and all my sins. Through the Most Precious Blood of your Son, Our Lord Jesus Christ, may you wash me clean in Holy Confession of the innocent blood that I spilled, blood that stains my body and my soul and the fragile life I've taken. May I make amends, atone for the rest of my life, and combat abortion in society with all available Providential means.

Oh, my most dear child, forgive me for having killed you. I entrust you to the most loving hands of the Father, Son, and Holy Spirit, through whose goodness you continue to exist. *Through Jesus Christ, Our Lord,* **Amen.**

---

† As regards *children who have died without Baptism,* the Church can only entrust them to the mercy of God, as she does in her funeral rites for them. Indeed, the great mercy of God who desires that all men should be saved, and Jesus' tenderness toward children which caused Him to say: "Let the children come to me, do not hinder them," allow us to hope that there is a way of salvation for children who have died without Baptism. "Limbo" is not a doctrine of faith however it is a common Catholic teaching among theologians, as noted by the International Theological Commission, in its study, *The Hope of Salvation for Infants Who Died Without Being Baptized,* approved by the Holy Father on Jan. 19, 2007. All the more urgent is the Church's call not to prevent little children coming to Christ through the gift of holy Baptism *(Catechism of the Catholic Church,* 1261).

"The life of a Christian is nothing but a perpetual struggle against self; there is no flowering of the soul to the beauty of its perfection except at the price of pain."

~ **St. Pio of Pietrelcina**

Merciful Compassion
Chapter 5

T he Lord gives us a chance for every blessing.

Recall how St. John Mary Vianney consoled a woman whose husband committed suicide by jumping off a bridge. St. Vianney told the woman that through her prayer and example, God granted her husband a special grace at the very last instant. Between the bridge and the water, like a moment in eternity, he converted and was sorry.

This story you're about to read involves such an instant, and many others throughout the lives of a mother, 69, and her daughter, 40. Through prayer and intercession, through trial, endurance, contrition, and blessing, each found healing, conversion, redemption. They still pray and struggle. But through the constant struggle against self, they have recognized God's hand in their lives, even in their earliest days.

Faith is a flower in their field.

As Blessed Teresa of Calcutta wrote about faith, and hope, that Christ encourages us to this lively confidence: *"Therefore I tell you, whatever you ask in prayer, believe that you have received it, and it will be yours"* (Mark 11: 24).

The apostle Peter also commands us to throw all cares upon the Lord, Mother Teresa reminds us. "And why should God not care for us since He sent us His Son and with Him all? Saint Augustine says: 'How can you doubt that God will give you good things since He vouchsafed to assume evil for you?'

"This must excite in us confidence in the providence of God who preserves even the birds and the flowers. Surely if God feeds the young ravens which cry to Him, if He nourishes the birds which neither sow nor reap nor gather into barns, if He vests the flowers of the field so beautifully, how much more will He care for men whom He has made in his own image and likeness and adopted as His children, if we only act as such, keep His commandments, and always entertain a filial confidence in Him."

While faith as a child of God—which we receive through the sacramental waters of Baptism—is required for the type of healing and conversion described in this story, healing and conversion also demand a process. In the Church and biblically, those who were healed were people of great faith, with tremendous trust in God.

But they paid a price, sacrificially, because healing requires time; cost, effort; and emotional, physical, and mental sacrifice. Often, there's a pilgrimage aspect to healing, through acts of reparation, charity, prayer, and devotion. That's why miracles happen at holy places like Lourdes or Guadalupe or Medjugorje. The time, energy, and the submission to His holy will become sacrificial.

During Jesus' time, the Syrophenicians offered another sort of sacrificial fire. At the southeastern corner of Jerusalem, they'd sacrifice children to demons, notably to the god, Moloch *(see Leviticus 18:21; 20:2-5; Kings 11:7; Isaiah 30:33; 57:9; Jeremiah 32:35; Acts 7:43).* The Syrophenicians were reprehensible to the Jews, who thought they were beasts, dogs even.

So it's paradoxical that a Syrophenician woman begged Christ to heal her child.

Remember what Jesus, in Tyre, told the woman, whose daughter was severely possessed by a demon: *"Let the children first be fed, for it is not right to take the children's bread and throw it to the dogs."* Imagine Jesus saying that? Imagine if I as a priest said that to someone who came to me for healing? *It's not right to give the bread of children to dogs.*

But she was desperate and humble, and so she had a humble prayer: *"Yes, Lord, yet even the dogs eat the crumbs that fall from their masters' table."* Do you see the humility? The faith?

"I have learned to be humble through humiliation, Father," is something Mother Teresa told me when I met her in Calcutta in 1994.

"When you face humiliation," said this tiny woman, who washed her garment in a bucket each day, "you should embrace it. Because we become one with Jesus, in His humiliation. We become one with the suffering of Christ."

The Syrophenician woman was being tested and humiliated. Listen to the Lord: *"O woman, great is your faith! Be it done for you as you desire."* Her daughter was healed instantly. But it was a difficult process for that woman to get to our Lord, to see Him. Syrophenicia was distant, 200 miles from Jerusalem. She must have spent days, maybe weeks, to get there. Imagine if you traveled weeks on foot or by donkey to see me and I treated you as Jesus did, even to test you. How many people could take that?

Extraordinary grace is inspired by humility. That type of faith cannot be explained. Nearly everyone would have had a negative reaction to Our Lord's statement unless he or she had a supernatural belief in God and Christ. That's why the Syrophenician woman received a miracle. She arrived at that faith and humility by supernatural merit.

That's true, too, of the mother and daughter who share their story here. Their story is raw, visceral. It's humiliating. It's profound. They convey their story with great humility. And yet, their testimony attests to God's power to heal people despite their circumstances.

Whether you're careening over a bridge in life or diving headfirst into an addiction, testimony like this sends a message of hope, inspiration, and liberation. This is a moving story that testifies to the power of priestly intercession, priestly blessing. After all, from the Patriarchs to the Apostles and beyond, the Church has encouraged its priests to bless the faithful, whether in person, in pictures, or in objects.

When I blessed a picture of this faith-filled woman's daughter, I could feel the Lord peeling off her bondages, breaking them open. I felt with great confidence that the Lord would heal her and set her free. I could feel the very strong faith of a desperate mother, pleading for her daughter, just like the Syrophenician woman.

This story shows, too, how generational patterns or sinful behaviors can mold a child. Even though a child's temperament and character may be different from a parent's, generational sin can perpetuate itself. And yet, grace overcomes behaviors and heals nature's imperfections. Grace heals. Grace sanitizes. *Grace sanctifies.*

Oftentimes, God allows us—He gives us free will—to have the power to destroy ourselves … or to reform. But we may have to hit bottom or even, tragically, lose a loved one to open a door to transformation through God's grace. Often, addictions, *and they are present here throughout four generations,* are so psychologically and emotionally crippling that they affect free will.

And yet, *up until that last microsecond before death,* we should never despair, because a soul can always turn toward the Lord. These words alone will give hope to the adopted daughter of Christ in this portrait of mercy, whose final cure comes at great cost.

These two lives ache with tragedy but overflow with hope and thanksgiving. These women participated in the Lord's Pascal Mystery, suffering, and death. Where there is suffering and death, God draws new life through the almighty power of His Son's Resurrection.

With each passing tragedy, through faith, we can grow thankful. For these two beautiful souls, the cumulative effect provides a tremendous witness to hope and to God's compassion.

They are the vested flowers of the field.

Ruth Begins the Story

What's amazing is that I lived at all. I was the second daughter in a family of four children. Father was a paper mill worker and mother took in ironing. He was a heavy drinker, and there were plenty of fights. After a big fight, we always ran to Auntie Lydia's. She was the safe zone. That was how we lived.

We were Catholic and I went to a Catholic school because my mother's mother paid for it. But when I was 12, I started smoking and drinking. By the time I was 15, I was brought before the courts and sent in 1955 to a home for juvenile delinquents run by nuns. I lived there 22 months, and that's where, probably for the first time in my life, I felt really safe.

After I got out, I graduated from the Catholic school in 1958. Things hadn't gotten much better at home; my mother divorced my father. She decided we'd have a good old time, so although I tried to be good, it didn't work. I went back to drinking and running around, this time with my mother.

Most mothers get mad at their daughters for sleeping around, but she wanted me to be promiscuous; I didn't want to be. It was a dysfunctional life.

I got into trouble with the police. I was picked up for drunken driving and served 90 days in jail, and then I served another 30 days for disorderly conduct. I was on probation for a year.

I took off with my cousin and another guy and ended up a few states away. In between, I was raped once. I also was gang raped. I had nothing to do with a man after the gang rape until I got married.

I met my husband, Nathan, in jail. He was serving time for drunk driving and driving without a license. In six months we were engaged, and married within a year by Fr. George, Nathan's uncle. We've been married nearly 50 years. But when we married, alcohol was still part of our life. And it continued to get worse. I left him six times and I divorced him once. We ended up back together. I blamed everything on him. I never looked at my own character defects, or my own drinking.

After he left, I was still having problems. I didn't have him to blame. I woke up one day on the couch, and I didn't remember how I got home. I had five little kids looking down at me. And I couldn't get up. That was in 1971, so our eldest was 11.

I told Nathan I wanted to quit drinking and go to AA meetings, and I haven't had a drink since that day. I started my sober years. But as the kids grew up, the oldest got into drugs and alcohol but went into treatment and has been sober since.

When my daughter Sara was five, they thought she had cystic fibrosis, but when I told them to test again she didn't have it.

She grew up in a household where no one drank. She was a cheerleader. She was in the chorus. She did all the things I was happy to see her do. But she started drinking in high school, and then she got pregnant when she was 15, and the boy 14.

She was 16 when she had her first child, Caleb. She stopped seeing the boy but wanted to keep the baby and we said we'd support her. She finished high school and then lived with us.

She met her future husband, Ben, and got pregnant again by him. And when she graduated from a one-year professional college, she had her second child, Debra. I also learned she was taking drugs. Ben physically abused her. He broke her rib and strangled her almost to death.

Sara Continues the Story

Sara   I had a good childhood. I felt really loved. Because I was the last of five children, I got plenty of attention. When I was diagnosed with cystic fibrosis, the doctor said I wasn't going to live to be 12. I think there were lots of prayers. I look at that as a miracle now. God was working on me a long time ago. I adored my parents. My brothers and sisters were great to me. When I was a teenager, that's when things started to go crazy. My parents were both recovering alcoholics, living a good, clean life, but I was looking for excitement. I had my first drink when I was 10 and started drinking a lot when I was 14. And smoking pot. But when I had my son when I was 16, I was off everything.

I barely made it through high school. I was too busy partying. When Ben and I moved to another state, I was exposed to all kinds of new drugs. The drinking continued. Ben got a job in still another state so we moved again. We would party and drink in front of our son, who was 2. When I left Ben and came back to be with my parents, he followed me. We started partying again.

Ben was involved in the occult. Before I met him, he got arrested for digging up a grave. He never told me what he would have done with the body. I can imagine not something good. A friend gave us a book, the *Necronomican*. It had spells in it and different chants to cast evil spirits on other people. One night we were reading out of it, and I remember sitting in a hotel room and laughing and joking and reading. I stored some stuff at my mom's house and for some reason, a box was open and my dad saw the book there. The book had a pentagram on it. When my dad saw it, he threw it in the wood stove and the chimney caught on fire. Dad put it out.

One night, Ben got violent, five hours of really intense abuse. It was pretty scary. I got away, went to my parents' house. He came over. And my parents said I needed to leave this guy and be done with him. They said if I left him they would sign me up for college. But he had this way of just schmoozing. I used to think, *"How can I go back with a guy who beat me up? I must be an idiot."* But these guys have a way about them. When they're nice, there's nobody nicer.

Then I got pregnant with my third child, a boy, Jason. And I graduated from college. Ben got another job offer and we moved out of state again. But the drinking problems returned. When Jason was a month old, I left Ben again and lived with my parents for a year.

I was doing good. I had three kids. *I was 21.* I wasn't drinking or using drugs. I was just starting to get it back together.

And then Ben returned and worked his masculine charm on me. We got back together. And things quickly got back to where they were. Except this time I was sober and I was living with this guy who was still drinking. I started going back to church.

One night—I was 22 or 23—I was crying: "My life is miserable, God!"

I was in a desperate place in my marriage and finances, just desperate, feeling sad and depressed. I was driving alone and I remember crying to God: "Sweep me off my feet! I need you! If you are really out there, I need you!" Like Gideon in Judges 6 who put out wet fleece to test God. And God just swept me off of my feet. *It was like a lightning bolt.*

I experienced such a joy and a peace and commitment to my marriage. God put some incredible people in my life after that. He showed me the different gifts of the Spirit. I remembered the sense of being able to withstand anything with the peace I had in my heart. I haven't had an experience like that ever again. That overriding sense of peace sustained me for 10 years. I knew that God was real. I'll never doubt again. It almost was like he was sitting in the car with me.

I remember crying and raising my hands to God, probably not safe while driving, but I was worshiping him, knowing in my heart that everything was going to be OK somehow. I committed myself to being a good wife and mom. What does God say about being a good wife and mom? And the Bible came alive to me. I would ask a question, look, and the answer would be there. It was incredible. I was in love with God. I was in love with Him. It just emanated from me.

Ben started to get into the things of God, too, and together, we were eating up God's word.

But then the devil's always there. We moved again. We lived separate lives. The kids and I, and Ben. He kept the drinking separate. He would come home that way, but it wasn't in the home like before. Then he got hurt on the job —a bad back injury. He wasn't able to work. We were living off workers' comp. I suggested that I go to work, but he said that's not what a woman is supposed to do. He said he wanted to get away and go out west. We moved there, sight unseen. Ben was still drinking and using prescription pills.

I remember him saying, "I'll never quit drinking. I will drink until the day I die." But I wasn't using. After that experience with God, I didn't want to have anything to do with it. I got extremely self-righteous with it actually: I don't use and you do. I went to the other extreme. The kids and I were going to church every week.

Ben went hunting one day and he said, "OK, God, I'll go to church and maybe you will bless me with a deer." He went to church. And the next day, he went hunting, and he got one at daybreak. And he went back at night and got another one. That was his experience with God. God swept him off his feet.

(Sobbing.)

For a year, it was like Heaven in our house! Everything was just changed—peace and kindness. He was so into God! So much so that when we would go somewhere he would leave the Christian radio station on because he wanted praises to come from our house 24 hours a day. He read the whole New Testament in two days. He was on fire. He poured all the booze down the drain. Two weeks before he had said, "I'll never stop drinking until I die!"

We had quite a few years that were really good. We held a Bible study in our house for over a year; we had a core group of 10 people. Ben and one of his friends played guitar, we all sang and prayed and were into the Bible study.

I got pregnant with the twins after that, after he had this experience. We named them Faith and Hope. That shows where our hearts were, really. Ben was able to go back to work without any medicine. We were able to buy some land and a new mobile home. It was our first house ever. Things were going great.

It went on for about eight years. But the business of life happened. The Bible study dwindled. The same people didn't come. Maybe it was kind of our laziness, having it at our house all the time instead of taking up the offer to have it at someone else's house.

Then Ben started getting sick. He learned he had thyroid problems—Grave's disease. His back was getting bad again, so he began taking pain medication. He had to quit his job. He couldn't do anything physically. Then he got another job but kept getting sicker, and he was laid off. I suspect they knew he was drinking.

Then I heard about the department of vocational rehabilitation and because of his back and the Graves disease, he qualified for it. They help disabled people become employable. I put together a business plan for a maintenance and cleaning company. It started good. He was still in pain but we had something to do. For a little while we were OK in the business. Then it got to be too much for him physically. He got sick real easy and his back seemed to hurt more than normal. A lot of times, he couldn't do anything. We got a big client but he was not able to keep up. I tried to take as many jobs as I could, but took too many.

That's when I started taking pills.

I started with a narcotic pain reliever that Ben used, and I moved up from there. Most people go to sleep; I'd get revved up. I remember going three days in a row without sleeping. It progressed over four years. Soon, I found I needed them to get out of bed in the morning. I quit all my jobs. I went on public assistance for close to a year. And I never did anything to change.

I was just always trying to find money to buy drugs. We hocked everything we could. We made it for a year doing that. Then I decided to work in the laundry area of a hospital. I did that for six months.

I started work at 4 a.m. so I needed pills for that. I always had an excuse. I did my work, and I don't think anyone suspected anything. Then I quit the hospital to go to work at a big retail store.

I worked a year there and thought I could make it there, all the while thinking, "I've got to get off this stuff. Other people get on without it." I paid rent and bought minimal food. The cars were always on empty. Everything was always broken down. But we had drugs every day. Ben still wasn't working. It was going down, down, down. I had to supply my habit and his and the habits were getting bigger and bigger as the days went by. We were snorting, because it affects you much quicker. I started missing days of work. If I didn't have anything, I couldn't function. The withdrawal is bad. You're freezing, but you're sweating. Your whole body shakes. I always felt like I wanted to crawl out of my skin. Your thoughts race like crazy.

A lot of the time I wanted to die. And I was only 35.

Ruth Asks God for Help

In February 2005, when I was 64, I had to have open-heart surgery. My lungs collapsed. I had transfusions. I couldn't get my strength back. In the hospital, I kept saying, "Help me God! Help me God! Help me God!"

When I got home, I wanted to say the Rosary. I said it over and over. Something changed in me because that was the first time I really turned to God and meant it. I had prayed at other times but never seemed to feel any connection. Except for the time that I was with the nuns for 22 months, it was the first time I felt something inside of me. I do not know what it was spiritually. I had no connection with the Holy Spirit at the time. They taught me that, but I had no concept of it.

I can't explain what happened to me in the hospital. I just know it was something wonderful. When I recovered, Nathan took me to my sister's and she cared for me. I started saying the Rosary every night. Every night I just had this feeling, "I've got to pray."

When I went to Mass, I felt nicer. I felt better. Lent was coming. I never did anything for Lent, but I wanted to go to Mass every day.

An old friend of mine, a holy lady, told me about a prayer group on Tuesday nights, so I started that. They had perpetual Eucharistic Adoration nearby and I started going. They needed someone to help in a little religious-articles store, connected to where the Eucharist was, so I began volunteering. I got acquainted with these women and started going back to AA. That was my life.

I learned about you, Father Machado. You were going to be at a church about two hours away. We went and were early, and I didn't care. Before, if I had to sit in a church for two hours, forget it. Now I loved it. I was so happy there. I brought Sara's picture along. That was in July 2006. I felt she was in danger of losing her life. And she had five kids.

I'm sure you remember, but I told you I would like you to bless my daughter, Sara. And you blessed me and I fell back. I rested in the Spirit. It was the most beautiful feeling I've felt in my life. I cried. The church was packed. It was so beautiful. The way you Consecrate the Eucharist, when you raise the Host, I never saw anything like that in my life. How reverent you are. If only all priests Consecrated the Eucharist that way. Now I am so much more aware of how sacred the Eucharist is.

After that, I called Sara. I asked her, "Did you feel anything different last night?" She said, "No, not really." But Sara really started running into trouble after that. She was gradually going downhill. It got much worse.

She had nothing there to hang on to.

Sara Finds Deliverance

By October 2005, I had quit going to church. I worked on Sundays because Sunday was time and a half. How can I sin and go to church, too?

During that time I could justify it to support my husband who was sick and taking care of the kids. I was in it for me, for the escape of the drugs.

I remember going through withdrawals and dreaming about going to treatment and being free of drugs. I thought:"Who will take care of everyone and keep up the house ? If I leave, what happens?" So I'd call my dealer and keep on going.

My mom was praying for me. I would give her bits and pieces but never the whole story. She called me after she went to see Father Machado and told me about her experience. I was really excited for her.

But life was getting bad. Everything got worse. It was about that time I had a walking nervous breakdown. I thought I would be divinely healed. I didn't want to use drugs or drink and I thought maybe God could take it away. But if you think you're in the depths, it can get worse. I got so low, I had an affair to get drugs.

After that, I remember looking through the carpet for little pieces of drugs. I didn't care. I became like an animal. Just low.

So I didn't get my miracle that way.

But God works in ways that aren't our ways. My oldest boy had moved out. He was 21 and had been on his own a few years. He was doing OK. He had his own place and a girlfriend. He drank, but was repulsed by drugs. He'd gone to the treatment center to see if my insurance would cover my treatment. And he went to talk to a social worker. He asked what he could do to get custody from someone for their kids, someone using drugs.

He presented all that to me. I just broke down. *"Oh, thank God! I am so ready to be done! I am so proud of you! You don't know the misery I've been in! I didn't know God would send you!"* He took the twins. My other two were in high school. I went into a 10-day treat-ment. You don't realize how far out of control it gets until your child comes to you, and that wasn't his job. But God bless him for doing that! God bless him, he saved my life!

Ruth's Healing Balm

Ruth   After Caleb called the treatment center and said he would take her, he called me. She was there 10 days and then was supposed to be released. She said she would like me and her father to be there when she got out. We drove two days to get there. She was diagnosed with post traumatic stress syndrome. She was like a person who has been in a war for 20 years. We got there before she was released and they let us in to see her. Ben was there, all drugged up, and he was falling asleep. The counselor said, "No one can go back into the home with him and stay sober."

So Sara agreed she would stay at the vacation home of one of her past clients, who said we could stay there a month for free.

When she got discharged, Ben was there, and he started carrying her luggage to his car.

Her father said, "Sara, what did the counselor just get done telling you?"

She said, "Well we could just have coffee."

He said, "Fine, you go have coffee, we're getting in the car and going home."

She got the baggage and put it in our car.

So we stayed with her in the cabin. She went back to work. The plan was I would stay with her a month, Nathan would go home, and I would see how things went. Ben was over there all the time, begging, crying, and saying he was going to go to meetings and treatment. Then he'd show the marks where he shot up.

All I could do was pray.

The cabin has a circular stairway. Sara tripped and had to go to the emergency room, and then she couldn't go back to work. I said to God, "Why are you doing this?" But all of a sudden, I understood: She had to come home with us. Jason was 16, Debra was 17, and they were both in high school. They wouldn't come. So we left with the twins. They were 9 years old at the time.

Sara's first day of sobriety was Oct. 23, 2007.

Sara's Loss

Sara   I did ask God for help when I had to make that decision to leave Ben and go with my parents. My dad was right. If I needed to stay sober, I needed to get in the car with them. I knew when I went with them that everything would be all right. It was a really hard decision, leaving my other two kids in the house. It was almost like leaving my whole life behind.

On Nov. 25, I went to an AA meeting to get my 30-day chip, and I came home and was driving into the garage and my brother and my sister were there. They told me Jason was dead. And it was from an overdose. The minute it happened, I thought it was so unfair, I wanted to scream: *"Jason's dead! Jason's dead!"*

But I had to decide: It was either fall apart or get really mad at this monster that took my life and took my boy.

Through prayer and the Holy Spirit, I learned instinctively that I would know how to handle a situation that before would have baffled me, because there was a power greater than me guiding me. Through that I got through my son's memorial service. I prayed every second. I know a force was holding me up that week. I didn't have thoughts of using. And I was back in my using stomping grounds, just a month sober.

That's got to be divine. That would have been a reason to use if there ever was one. If I was happy I would use. If it was sunny, I would use. If it was rainy, I would use. I always had a reason.

*This gave me a reason **not** to use.*

Ruth's Discovery

My son and Sara bought airline tickets and left the next morning. Nathan and I and our two other daughters, with the twins, drove 29 hours in snowstorms to join them. We learned that on the day Jason died, Ben went to get Jason's paycheck. And then he went to his bank to get his savings. One of the drugs they found in Jason's body was a drug Ben used to shoot up with.

Sara's Confession

While in treatment, I had talked to a counselor, but my brother suggested going to this wonderful Catholic Church, this shrine, for Confession. When I went up the hill, I had this feeling of awe. It was fall. It's a long walk to get to the actual chapel. You go through different corridors. You can hear the wind on the side of the building. It's a feeling of awe that God is gently, but powerfully, there. I knew I was going up to open my heart and confess. Maybe I was finally ready to meet Him. Being in God's holiness, you feel like dirty rags. You feel unworthy.

I realized how big God is.

The priest wasn't judgmental, and I was expecting him to be. He was gentle and compassionate and almost proud of me, that I came in there.

After Mass, they have a place where you can go and pray. And the place where you walk in is all crutches and canes that people left because they were healed. What a testimony to see those little ones from children and to think of all the people healed in that chapel. Walking in, you think you're not going to walk out the same after you see something like that. I looked at those and thought, "Wow! I left a mental crutch there."

After you are cleansed like that ... it's just *"I'm free! I'm free!"*

It was the same in my mom's life. The love in her. She was always loving. Even when she knew I was using, she was always accepting. To overlook the sins of somebody, that gift is not of this world. I know something incredible happened to my mom, and she passed it on to me.

Ruth's Prayer for Sara

Ruth   I believe the blessing from God, through you, Father Muchado, healed her addiction. I just know when you prayed over that picture, something happened to change the play for the devil. And it changed to God's way. That's my feeling. That's my testimony.

I only know that my daughter is alive and she should be dead with all that she's taken, and for some reason, I should have been dead, too. Because she was so abused, with no money, and having to leave the kids, she felt trapped, like a caged animal.

Once she knew she could go into treatment, she grabbed onto that like a hungry lion.

She's done everything she can to get well, I believe because of the prayers. I have been praying, in some way, for this girl for 20 years. I've seen her go to Hell and back. But it wasn't until I became more spiritual, until I knew how to pray, not just the "gimme, gimme" but the "Thy will be done" sort of prayers. And then finding you and believing you could help ... you are the vehicle the Lord is using.

Sara Holds on to Hope

I'm sure I am where I am because of my mother's intervention. You know I've had this thought: "If God had just taken my addiction away from me, it would not have stuck. I had to go through those bad times because I don't ever want to go back there again." I want to warn people: *Don't go there.* It'll not get better. It'll just get worse. With the help of God, that's the only way.

I get attacks in the night. It feels like evil, and I pray and it goes away. It's not a coincidence. That's the light of God shining in the darkness. And the darkness does not go away easily once it has its hands on you. I believe God has control of everything. ~⍺Ω

✝

Prayer for Generational Healing

We pray, Heavenly Father, in reparation for the sins of our ancestors, our current and future family lineage, for the repose of their souls. We offer our sufferings for the living and deceased. Heavenly Father, through the merits of Our Lord Jesus Christ's passion, death, and suffering, we offer up to you in amends, our supplication, intercession and our prayers for our loved ones, living or dead. We offer our heartfelt prayers for conversion and sanctification and purification, to bring deliverance of our dearly departed ancestors from venial and temporal punishments of sin, that they may enjoy eternal rest in the glory of Paradise. And as we offer our prayers, may we enter into deeper bonds of charity with them. May our familial communion grow more profound, and render their intercession for us more fruitful and effective.

We pray that living generations of our family be freed from mortal and venial sins and that they be brought to contrition and conversion, and that they make reparation, amends, and atone for their sins, that vice be uprooted, and that they avoid all near occasion of sin.

We pray that they make reparation for any scandal due to their sin, so that they may be called to great heights of holiness in the spirit of the Beatitudes, through the infusion of the theological, cardinal, and moral virtues. Heavenly Father, may they acquire increased supernatural merits of grace and increase their eternal reward. *Through Jesus Christ, Our Lord,* **Amen.**

Prayer for the Healing of Addiction

We pray that the Lord may deliver us from every addiction—physical, mental, moral, emotional, psychological—including addictions to alcohol, sex, gambling, pornography, or harmful substances.

We pray that the Lord grant us spiritual discipline and mastery, a spirit of mortification and asceticism, clarity of vision, and firmness of purpose so that we may prevail over every temptation to these addictions by way of the world, of the flesh, and of the devil. And thereby escape the slavery of the old creature, wounded by Adam's sin, and become a new creation redeemed in Christ, Jesus, and so that through the virtuous gifts of sobriety, prudence, moderation, and fortitude, we may be spiritually transformed and liberated, to great heights of sanctity. *Through Jesus Christ, Our Lord,* **Amen.**

"At times the Cross appears without our looking for it: it is Christ who is seeking us out. And if, by chance, before this unexpected Cross which, perhaps, is therefore more difficult to understand, your heart were to show repugnance . . . don't give it consolations. And, filled with a noble compassion, when it asks for them, say to it slowly, as one speaking in confidence: 'Heart: heart on the Cross! Heart on the Cross!'"

~ **St. Josemaría Escrivá,**
The Way of the Cross

A Heart on the Cross

Chapter 6

E very contact a priest has with his people should draw the priest to the Creator, and bring him greater self-awareness as he becomes Christ in the world. And his heart should beat for Christ.

Christ consecrated priests to be His ambassadors and prophets to people of all faiths, or even of no faith. Let me write as if to my brethren priests for a little while here. We're not functionaries with liturgical roles. We're shepherds of *all* souls and need to tend to them. Do we shy away from the world? Why? We always need to be missionaries, even as diocesan priests. We must go out to the people, to proclaim Christ!

After all, you, my brothers, represent the heart of God, which burns with compassion, as Pope Benedict XVI noted in his June 19, 2009, homily, as he inaugurated the *Year for Priests*. A heart not unlike in nature as the heart he venerated that same day, a relic of the saintly Curé of Ars. "A heart that blazed with divine love," the Holy Father said, that "experienced amazement at the thought of the dignity of the priest, and spoke to the faithful in touching and sublime tones, telling them that 'after God, the priest is everything!' ... Only in Heaven will he fully realize what he is."

The same heart, the heart of St. Vianney, preserved all these years after *dies natalis* on Aug. 4, 1859, was brought to a parish in Merrick, Long Island, N.Y., named after him, the Curé of Ars parish. The pastor, Fr. Charles Mangano, told me he had written to the Bishop of Belley-Ars to ask if the heart of the great saint could be brought there so the faithful could venerate it, pray before it briefly, and in 2006 his request was granted. The saint's heart liquefies at times, and I recall an earlier instance when our Holy Father, then Cardinal Joseph Ratzinger, was praying before the heart, venerating it with a group of people, and it started pumping, moving! *Can you imagine?*

So the heart of the pastor of Ars came to Long Island, and drew the attention of ABC, NBC, and CBS because more than 15,000 pilgrims in all lined up for a moment of prayer while gazing at this great saint's heart, his priestly heart. Pilgrims also went to Holy Confession. And Fr. Mangano told me of the miracles that occurred—people cured of cancer and AIDS, from physical and psychological illness, demoniacs freed from harassment ... all from the heart of a priest who loved with his mind, his body, *his soul*. Imagine what your priest's heart can achieve, in Christ. Imagine what your own heart can achieve, in Christ.

An archdiocesan priest in northern New Jersey, the late Fr. Thomas A. Gillick, related this to a parishioner in a letter, after celebrating the 50th year of his priesthood: "The priesthood is a mystery to even those who share it, a mystery emphasized every time the Words of Consecration are said, or Absolution given, or an effort made by teaching or preaching to reach into the depths of the human soul; to enlighten it, to move the human will, and so many other ways. It is God's work and we must be content to be instruments, leaving it to the Divine Knowledge whether on any given occasion we are good instruments, or not so good, or even bad. The Lord has called us. And the only thing we can do is to try to respond day by day, occasion by occasion. Truly the task is too awesome for any man, but the Lord has willed it anyway, and so we keep trying. ... "

Not of This World

Priests gain tremendous peace, joy, and happiness when they realize *who* they really are. How they're called to be instruments, privileged channels of Christ, celebrating His sacraments, giving blessings, and instructing the faithful on using sacramentals, reminders of the great gifts that bring the faithful to Heaven. Priests rejoice in their identity when they discover it, and that identity is a source of motivation to rededicate themselves and refocus their ministry toward Christ.

Who they are is obscured by their naturalistic, secular world, which hides the supernatural dimension. Yet the priesthood is spontaneous in its joy. A priest lives spontaneously in this world but isn't of this world. That's a paraphrase of St. John's gospel, and also the priesthood's modern challenge. Priests aren't called to be absorbed into the world.

We live *in* the world, but are not *of* the world. For priests who have grown weary in their vocation, or for those who've lost sight of the precious nature of their calling, they've yet to tap that thought, or grace.

Before Our Lord in the Garden of Gethsemane begged His Father to remove the chalice—if it was His will— He lifted His eyes up to Heaven and prayed, in what has been called a signature of St. Joseph, the "prayer of the custodian," for the priesthood, for the Apostolic Church, reminding His apostle priests that they would suffer as he suffered, but find joy fulfilling the mission of the Redeemer, fulfilling the will of His Father, and repeating, over and over, that they were *in* the world, not *of* the world *(John 17)*.

"And now I am no longer in the world, but they are in the world, and I am coming to you. Holy Father, protect them in your name that you have given me, so that they may be one, as we are one. While I was with them, I protected them in your name that you have given me. I guarded them, and not one of them was lost except the one destined to be lost, so that the scripture might be fulfilled. But now I am coming to you, and I speak these things in the world so that they may have my joy made complete in themselves. I have given them your word, and the world has hated them because they do not belong to the world, just as I do not belong to the world. I am not asking you to take them out of the world, but I ask you to protect them from the evil one. They do not belong to the world, just as I do not belong to the world. Sanctify them in the truth; your word is truth. As you have sent me into the world, so I have sent them into the world. And for their sakes I sanctify myself, so that they also may be sanctified in truth" *(John 17: 11-19)*.

It is all about love. Christ wants His joy *fulfilled* in ourselves, through love! He wants us to be sanctified in the truth, to go into the world, to be consecrated in the truth, as He is consecrated, He who is Christ.

Go to the Garden, my friends! Before Judas arrived, Jesus was praying so intensely His sweat turned to blood. By the grace of God, during pilgrimages to the Holy Land, I have prayed on that same rock, that rock made Sacred by the Lord Himself, by the blood He sweat, by His tears for ungrateful man. As I prayed on my hands and knees, as I prayed prostrate on this Rock of Agony, I could feel the force of power coming from this holy relic.

On the Rock of Agony, the Shepherd prayed for us, for His people, for His priests.

But the Lord went back—not once, twice. He needed the support, the help, of His apostles. The Lord is pleading with you: *Stay awake with me!* The shepherds of our parishes are good priests who care and are worthy of our support. These are the shepherds crying out—are you there for them? Do you fast and pray for them? Keep watch with them? Or do you take them for granted? Where do you stand for the Lord? Are you Peter? Judas? Are you in the crowd? The same crowd that welcomed Jesus into Jerusalem, who turned on Him and yelled: *"Crucify Him! Crucify Him?"* Who are you?

The Lord Is Here

Many people don't realize this, but Barabbas also was named Jesus. The crowd had a choice: Did they want Jesus of Nazareth, or Jesus Barabbas, whose last name combined two Aramaic words: *bar,* which means son, and *abba,* father. In other words, Jesus, son of the father. (The second part of the name also could be *rabbon,* for master or rabbi.)

The people chose another Jesus! Do you?

People of Christ, if our Lord came, and our Lord is present at every Holy Mass, would you be certain to arrive on time? Would you leave early? Or would you want the front pew? You wouldn't want our Lord to leave, would you? And yet, He is here, present in the Blessed Sacrament, in the Word of God, the Gospels, in Holy Communion, in the blessings from the beginning to the end of Holy Mass. When the priest leaves, it is our Lord leaving! You should be in tears that the Mass is over—but ready to take the Lord's message into the world, to proclaim the good news. You should want to help your shepherds, your priests, your pastors in their evangelical mission.

Pope John Paul II said the sign of a vibrant parish is vocations. Vocations are the fruit of the flower. Where prayer life and spirituality are dead, vocations shrivel up. If there are no young people to tap good soil, to take root, there's not much love for the Shepherd, for Jesus.

You come to church because you want something from God? You come to church to feel good?

Why do you run out of church when Mass is over? *The Lord is here!* Don't take your eye off the Shepherd. Look at the Lord on the Cross. Look! Look into His eyes. Let Him speak to your soul as He hangs there on the Cross. *Let Him speak to your heart!* And then you can be like a prodigal son or daughter and say, "Lord, I have offended heaven and I have offended you. I am no longer worthy to be called your son. I am no longer worthy to be your daughter. *Treat me as one of your slaves."* And like the prodigal son, mean it. It's a privilege, no, to be His slave and to serve Him, as the Shepherd?

Do you pray for the priest who baptized you, or the bishop who confirmed you, the priest who absolved you from your sins in your first Confession? Do you thank them in prayer? Do you pray for the priest who invoked God's blessing on your parents in the Sacrament of Holy Matrimony, without whose sacrifice you would have no life in the Church? Do you thank the priests who gave Viaticum to your grandparents, and the priest who ministered to one generation after another in your families?

Would you sell your Shepherd for 30 pieces of silver? As so many saints have said, we really get the priest we deserve. And if there aren't enough priests, or there are priests involved in scandals, where are the faithful who are praying? Where are the families on their knees, praying, fasting to high Heaven, praying for the sanctification of priests and the shepherds, crying for them, until they are like Jesus, the Son of God, on His knees, on the Rock of Agony, praying for the apostles, for the apostles who ran away from Him?

At the House of Caiaphas, after Peter denied the Lord, the Lord was led out, bound and in chains, and he looked at Peter. Their eyes met. Can you feel Peter shaking? Can you feel him remembering what the Lord told him, after he promised the Lord, "I'll die for you, Jesus?" Can you see in Jesus' eyes, recognition of Peter's own denial, and yet, love? Peter wept bitterly, because he had let his Shepherd down.

Shepherds: Serve Your Flock

How do we as shepherds let our people down?

Priests of our Lord and Savior Jesus Christ, do you always serve your flock? If you serve a rural parish, when you drive through the fields, day or night, do you beg the Lord to bless the families who own the farms with an abundant harvest? To bless them and help them realize this is all from God, thanking our Lord for the bounty of the land, the fields, the fruit of the Earth, through which man is able to live? Do you thank the Lord for blessing man with the ingenuity, the strength, the hope, the trust to rely on God's providence? Thanking, thanking, thanking God for all He has done, and asking for blessings on those who have abandoned themselves to God's providence?

When we consider Creation and its bounty, we're really trusting in God. This is the basis for a real spiritual life of trust. Do we ask God's blessing to preserve this creativity and productivity? To preserve the crops, because we realize the volatility of the elements—the wind, sun, rain, snow—and also their vulnerability to pestilence, disease, sickness, and harmful insects, to protect the fragile nature of the land and the farm animals? They're all subject to the slightest deviation from providential care.

Do we realize how fragile human existence is? We're fragile, held by a thread, and we realize this when we realize the land is from our Creator.

Everything these days seems to be man-made and artificial, even the economy. Yet people who live off the land and work the land are put into communion with the Creator in a particular way. Historically this always has been the case: People of greater faith live closer to the land. From the ancient Babylonians, or peoples living along the Jordan River, the Canaanites, or in Africa, to today, people who live in rural areas are more traditional-minded, and have a greater awareness of the sense of God. They turn to Him as a natural sentiment. Knowing their Creator is instinctual.

Creation is a reflection of the Creator. How have we as people and as priests gotten away from the "land," the traditions of our faith, and from all they point to?

St. Paul says to the Romans that in contemplating nature, we see our Creator. "For what can be known about God is plain to [men], because God has shown it to them. Ever since the creation of the world His eternal power and divine nature, namely, invisible though they are, have been understood and seen through the things He has made" *(Romans 1:19-20).*

It is the reflection, the contemplation of nature that turns us to God. It's the natural that brings us to the supernatural. It's the seemingly coincidental that brings us to the eternal.

If we, as priests, live out our priesthood, naturally, with a constant awareness of the divine, we transform our people.

Faith Overcomes Death

I recall from my days as a hospital chaplain in Ottawa, Canada, the tremendous effect of grace from chance meetings with patients, being content to be God's instrument on any given occasion. It showed me the power of Christ through the priesthood, and the power of blessing, and anointing. One case I'll never forget. It was around Easter time. In fact—this strikes me deeply on recollection, but there are no coincidences with God—it was the Feast of the Priesthood, Holy Thursday.

Two nurses told me one of their patients had died. He was a priest, Fr. Richard, who had served as a missionary in Latin America until his health broke down. He needed acute care, so he returned to his home archdiocese in Ottawa, Canada. He was in his 70s. He had a chronic illness, and all that day, his vitals plummeted—his skin color changed, his heartbeat was weak and irregular—he was in his final hour. Then, his brain function was diminishing; finally, his heart beat its last.

I had gone to the nursing station to document my visit, as I was official chaplain and the protocol required record of pastoral intervention.

I had administered Anointing of the Sick with Viaticum a few months prior, but I knew I also could anoint him conditionally, if I was able to do so within 10 to 15 minutes of his supposed death—as there usually is a window between "apparent medical death" and "absolute death"—separation of his soul from his body.

Therefore the Church has always permitted a conditional anointing in a case where a soul has not departed from the body.

I returned to the nursing station after Fr. Richard's final anointing. But a nurse soon ran down the hall after me: "He jumped out of bed!" She had been preparing his body for the mortician, and he leapt up, opening his eyes. "I was in shock!" she said. She told Fr. Richard that all his vitals seemed to show he had died. He said he was hungry. He didn't leave the hospital, but was healthier than he had been in years. Because of his chronic condition, he still required acute care. But he lived for two more years. †

See the power of the Church, the power of the Sacrament, not my own? It's incredible to say even the dead may be healed, restored, brought back to life. But these are signs of the Church. Christ said one of the signs would be that we would be able to raise the dead, heal people from demons. We have instances of this in the life of the mystics and saints, too.

I recall another case of a woman, 50 years old, in extremely advanced stages of breast and ovarian cancer. She was dying. I anointed her, and the doctor said her death was imminent. "She'll likely not last a day," he said. Yet, after the anointing, she revived. She got a burst of life and lived another nine months. *Praise and glory be to our Lord and Savior, Jesus Christ!*

Her recovery took the doctors aback. In fact, the doctors were stunned and became humbled. In private conversations they said it was a miracle, and they were more open to God. Publicly, they couldn't say what it was, but that it was scientifically and medically impossible.

Medical personnel seem like gods. They have a say over life and death. They're experts. They judge conditions and have a great gift to see the evolution of the disease or illness,

---

† **Author's note:** A person may be re-anointed if the person's situation has deteriorated. Moral theologians have allowed for conditional anointing, in the initial window of time when a person shows apparent signs of death, as the soul may not have yet separated from the body. Within a few minutes to an hour of apparent death, anointing is allowed. And, if the person has the intention of being contrite, even if they're unconscious, sins can be remitted. If they're unrepentant, they will, indeed, die that way.

and they can tell when a person is nearing the end. So they are very accurate in prognosis and diagnosis and the likelihood of death.

But some things cannot be explained.

In this story, doctors told Steve he had a serious heart condition, lung cancer, and Stage Four Chronic Lymphocytic Leukemia (CLL), for which there was no known cure at the time.

Doctors gave him eight years to live. But today, he expects many more. How? He received the best chemotherapy known to man: The spontaneous love of his Father, Our Father, and a brush with the Divine.

A missionary priest was passing by. And his invocations of St. Joseph, St. Stephen, and St. Raphael met with Steve's literal and spiritual conversion of heart. As he stood before the priest and received a simple blessing, God suddenly knew the urgency of His beloved son's need. In a moment of love, from Father to a son, the Lord immediately intervened in Steve's life.

"Oh, how great is the priest," said St. Vianney. *"If he realized what he is, he would die."*

Steve Begins His Story

Steve

At one time in my life, I decided there were "more important things to do," so I divorced and left the Church. I'm almost 70 now. I left the Church for 27 years.

I received an annulment, and then remarried in 1989, not in the Church. My new wife, Peggy, had been raised Catholic, but was away from the Church for 20 years. Peggy later received an annulment, too. What got us back to the

Lord was my brother-in-law, Jim. He was killed in a car accident in Georgia in 1995. We were living in Virginia. So we drove to the memorial service. And at the funeral we both heard in our hearts: "You need to get back to church."

Driving home, we didn't say anything to each other. But when we got back, I said, "Did you hear—? and she cut me off and said, "Yes! I heard the same thing!"

Three months after our marriage was blessed in the Roman Catholic Church on April 29, 1997, Peggy's son, Greg, was killed. He was drunk, ran through a red light, and plowed into a van. It was July 24, 1997.

If we had not returned to the Church, the grief would have been unbearable. But now we have the Sacraments and can cope better with the loss.

When Greg was killed, I walked out of my job and didn't look back. It was such a life-changing event that I realized work wasn't that important; family *was*. I was terrified of dying. I wouldn't accept dying as part of life until I started working for Maureen Flynn at *Signs & Wonders for Our Times* in Herndon, Va. And let me tell you, if you had told me about visionaries or miracles back then, I would've laughed at you. I just didn't believe in them.

The homilist at Greg's funeral told the story of a San Francisco bishop who was visiting a packed church, made up of wealthy and poor people. When he started his homily, a bum came in off the street, his hair all matted, and he smelled of whiskey. He shuffled pew to pew. And no one would give him a seat. Everyone shifted away. He walked around the church, and when he left, the bishop said, "Christ just walked by, and no one recognized Him."

Photo courtesy of the Meinberg family.
Steve and Peggy Meinberg, in 2008.

After the funeral, while in our hotel room—Peggy was sleeping—all of a sudden Greg was there, and someone I thought was the Lord, whose face was hidden by a bright light, so bright I couldn't look at it. I focused on Greg. Both of them were standing in front of me, offering me a chalice. I tried to sip from the chalice, but it scared the daylights out of me. Even after my conversion, I wasn't the greatest Catholic in the world. I didn't have the kind of faith to believe in visions.

When we flew back to Virginia, I said, "I need to talk to a priest." I didn't know what to do. I was shaken. I finally told Peggy what happened, in detail: Greg had a white robe with a cincture around him, white like I-can't-believe white. Peggy was more of a believer than I was. She wondered why the vision appeared to me and not her. I said, "Probably because I didn't believe that stuff."

We learned after Greg died, that he respected the homeless. He had all these people turn out for his funeral Mass, and we were astonished. We had no idea he had done so much with the homeless. He was not church-going. We didn't think he was close to Christ. Because of Greg's death, and seeing him and Jesus after, made me come back to the Church with a vengeance. We joined the Legion of Mary, and other prayer groups. We became active in a prison ministry on Saturdays and Sundays.

I was one of these "abortion-is-a-personal-decision" folks and, man, did our pastor, the late Monsignor James McMurtrie, really set me straight. He was wonderful. We ended up joining pro-life groups and we marched for life.

I started working with Peggy Hennessey, Maureen Flynn's mom, at *Signs & Wonders for Our Times,* a founder of the International Week of Prayer and Fasting at the National Basilica of the Immaculate Conception in Washington, D.C. My faith grew even more from working at *Signs & Wonders.* Peggy Hennessey and I worked in shipping and had a ball. I never really enjoyed work so much in my life, because it wasn't work. I was still working for Maureen when I was driving in my car one day, this is a year after Greg's funeral, and a voice from the back seat said: *"Greg would have given him a seat. Greg's in Heaven."* And I knew exactly what he was talking about—that bum in the church. I couldn't believe it.

I wasn't afraid of dying anymore.

Conversion of Heart

I have arterial fibulation, A-Fib. The upper chamber of my heart won't close, and it can lead to a stroke. In 2005, I had an A-Fib attack. I went to the hospital and spent the night. What happens is that if the medicine doesn't convert the heart rhythm, it may not convert on its own. I've be blessed that my heart valve has always closed, if not by medicine, then on its own, within 24 hours.

Because it converted, and the heart went back to its normal rhythm, the next morning they said I could leave. But then the doctor said, "you're not going anywhere, we have an internist who wants to talk to you." When the internist shared the results of a blood test, he said he thought I had CLL, chronic lymphoma. He ordered a CT scan to see if anything else was going on.

That's when they discovered something. They found a spot on the lower lobe of my right lung. But they didn't think it was anything to worry about, or that it was related to the CLL. Meanwhile, Peggy and I were getting ready for a Florida vacation.

In Florida, I got a call and they said I needed to get back to see an oncologist. "Wait," I said. "Just wait. We'll be back in a week and a half to two weeks." I wasn't worried.

When I got back, and saw the oncologist, he ordered a PET scan. It came back: You have lung cancer. "This is wonderful," I thought—leukemia *and* lung cancer. They did a biopsy. "Yeah, it's lung cancer." And by the way, they said there's no treatment, no cure for the CLL (one has been found since). They had said I had eight years to live, but now they believed the CLL was more advanced.

"I want you to see the surgeon immediately to get the lower part of the lung out," the doctor told me.

I said, "That's not happening." I'm a hard-headed German to start with. Do it my way, and if I die, I die. This is how I was thinking now. I'm going to International Week of Prayer and Fasting.

Prior to the Week of Prayer and Fasting, on Saturday, Oct. 7, 2006, on the Feast of the Most Holy Rosary, there was a youth conference at a gymnasium in a nearby church, St. Joseph's in Herndon, Va. Father, you celebrated Mass and gave the homily. Peggy Hennessey grabbed me in my seat. She took me right to you, Father. We'd never met before. She said: "Tell him what's wrong with you."

I said, "Father, I have leukemia and I have lung cancer."

So you started praying over me. It was so loud in the gym—kids were screaming, a band was playing—people asked me what saints you invoked, and I said, "I have no clue." When you put your hand on my forehead, I felt a warm heat, almost like a fire, not burning hot, but so warm, go all throughout my body and out my toes.

I've been prayed over many times and I never felt anything like that. And when you were through, I hadn't heard a word you said because of the noise. I turned to Maureen, who had come over, and my wife, and Maureen's mom, and I said, *"Don't ask me why I am saying this, but I don't think I have the cancer anymore."*

Dumbfounded Doctor

I had appointments with doctors when I came back, but the appointments canceled, and then two weeks later I was sitting in their offices. They took another scan. The doctor comes in and has this dumb look on his face. He looks down at the radiologist's report, the results from a second CT scan, which would precede lung cancer surgery, looks up at me, and I'm waiting for him to say something. He says: "We can't find the lung cancer." I had never seen such a dumb look on a doctor's face. I think he thought he had the wrong file. He looked up. He looked down. He looked up. *"We can't find the cancer."* Peggy and I were looking at each other. "The CLL is down to zero," he said. (They had done blood work, too.) "I can't explain it," he said. Peggy said, "Do you believe in prayer?"—we were at a Catholic hospital—and he says, "Well, yeah."

I thought about it: They said the CLL was down to zero and it had been Stage 4, no cure, no treatment.

To this day, they can't explain it. I went back every six months for a chest X-ray and blood work. Last year, the doctor told me I didn't need to see him for a year. He's amazed. *I'm* amazed.

For a long time, every time I told that story, I cried. It brought tears to my eyes. It was a feeling of joy, great joy.

When we visit relatives in California, we have a Rosary group there, and we meet after Mass. When this group of Filipino ladies heard the story, they wanted to touch me.

Others did too. Every time I fill out forms in a doctor's office, they want to hear how I'm doing. They go "Wow!" when they see what I've been through. "How are they treating you today for the cancer?" they ask. I answer, "I don't have cancer anymore." They look at me: "Excuse me?"

I still have my A–Fib and diabetes. I often think I wish I had told you about everything, Father. I have high blood pressure and arthritis, too, but let me tell you: I thank the Lord for you every day. You were the instrument and God did it through you.

Let's face it, even a lot of priests don't believe in that stuff today.

No Diagnosis Is Final

I met you Father, a year later at the next International Week of Prayer and Fasting, and I remember thanking you, kissing your hands. I did it because I know that the way people treat priests today is an abomination, it's unbelievable. I wanted to respect your priesthood, and who you are as a person. A year later, you flew into town and came to dinner. I was so grateful!

I don't think people should ever give up. People come down with cancer and they blame God. That's stupid. They should never give up. When I was diagnosed, I had progressed in my Faith, so it didn't bother me that much. Peggy was more upset than I was. Life goes on. If God wants to take me, that's life. It just never upset me at that point. Don't get me wrong. After the healing when I got back and this doctor is telling me "We can't find your cancer," I had tears in my eyes. But those were tears of joy. But it was not a situation of crying out, going, "Oh Lord!" Life goes on. Maybe my faith was stronger than I thought it was. I wasn't looking to be healed. I was sort of thrown into it.

My CLL is still at zero, and the lung cancer hasn't returned. I give thanks every day.

I love the Church. The older I get, the more I love it. We have the "Pink Sisters" here in St. Louis, MO. The nuns of the Congregation of Holy Spirit Adoration Sisters, who wear a rose-colored habit, adore Christ in the Eucharist 24 hours a day every day; perpetual Eucharistic Adoration. Almost every day I go to their church and pray with them. The first part of my Adoration is always Thanksgiving. That's at the top, my healing. And I'm thankful that we have priests like you,

Father. You have extended my life and I love you for it.~Ω

✝

Prayer for Fortitude

Divine Savior, as you exercised the cardinal virtue of fortitude, you inspire us unceasingly to share your Cross through life's tempestuous seas, the vicissitudes of this life, and the trials of our earthly pilgrimage. Oh Lord, in my human frailty, I often buckle before the burden of afflictions; without you, I can do nothing; with you, I may do everything. Always endow me with the effervescent boldness of your Holy Gospel. *Through Jesus Christ, Our Lord,* **Amen.**

Prayer for Healing from a Terminal Illness

Like the Gospel woman suffering from hemorrhage, I too, Lord Jesus, wish to touch the hem of your garment. Like the Roman centurion, I am not worthy that you should come under my roof, but only say the word and I shall be healed. May your Most Sacred Body strengthen my body ravaged by illness. May your Most Precious Blood in the Holy Eucharist purify the contagion in my blood. Revitalize me, oh Lord with hope, as I am forlorn and dying. You are my rock, my fortress, my refuge. In you is my only hope for salvation and healing. With expectant faith, I make up, as St. Paul says, in my body, what's lacking in the sufferings of Christ for the salvation of souls, knowing that if it be possible, that I be cured from this terminal illness. Nonetheless, not my will but Your Holy Will be done. *Through Jesus Christ, Our Lord,* **Amen.**

> *"Breathe into me, Holy Spirit, that my thoughts may all be holy. Move in me, Holy Spirit, that my work, too, may be holy. Attract my heart, Holy Spirit, that I may love only what is holy. Strengthen me, Holy Spirit, that I may defend all that is holy. Protect me, Holy Spirit, that I may always be holy."*
>
> *~ St. Augustine*

A Face for Christ

Chapter 7

D o you seek the face of Christ? Where do you find Him? Are you like Solomon of old, who wrote of the Nuptial Feast, evidenced in the Mystical Rose, the relationship between God and man, joined by love through the priest?

"I sought him whom my soul loves; I sought him but found him not. I called him, but he gave no answer. I will rise now and go about the city, in the streets and in the squares; I will seek him whom my soul loves. I sought him, but found him not. The sentinels found me, as they went about in the city. ... they beat me, they wounded me, they took away my mantle, those sentinels of the walls. I adjure you, O daughters of Jerusalem, if you find my beloved, tell him this: I am faint with love" (Song 3, 5, 8).

Christ is sick with love, willing to give His Body as our bread, His Blood, as our wine. Do you recognize Christ as the apostles did in the breaking of the bread *(Luke 24:35)*?

In *The Priest Is Not His Own (© 2004, Ignatius Press)*, Servant of God Archbishop Fulton Sheen wrote, "Each time that priests 'break bread' during the Mass, not only will they recognize the sacrifice of Christ for them, as did the disciples at Emmaus, but also He will recognize them. Not unbroken bread, not unbroken bodies will the High Priest accept from our hands. Was not the wheat already broken to become bread? Were not the grapes already crushed to become wine? Even nature suggests victim hood as inseparable from the priesthood of offering bread and wine at table."

The priest is the Icon of Christ. Think of Christ on the Way of the Cross, gifting Veronica with His image for her kindness, now preserved by the Vatican for the Ages. The name Veronica—*vera icon*—means *true icon*. We priests— through the Sacrament of Holy Orders—are called to be true icons, true reflections, of Christ. But unlike the image of Christ, the physical image that sits miraculously above the fabric fibers that make up Veronica's Veil, is Christ Himself, Christ the Head, sacramentally joined to the fabric of our souls, the fabric of our very being. Just as the Veil is more than a physical imprint of Christ, the priest himself becomes an instrument of Christ, of how He works. The priest reflects His image.

When the priest blesses, it is Christ who blesses. When the priest anoints, it is Christ who anoints. When the priest consecrates, it is Christ who consecrates. At Holy Mass, Christ is one with the priest—priest, victim, and altar of sacrifice. An indelible mark has been imprinted on the soul through the Sacrament of Holy Orders. One is a priest forever, in Heaven, in Purgatory and even—God forbid—Hell.

The priest, if he's faithful to his calling, is destined to live out his priesthood in union with Christ the High Priest, in the glory of Heaven. However, the priest has free will, just as the angels did at the beginning of their creation. Just as Lucifer and many angels rebelled and fell despite their great beauty and splendor, so too may a priest betray his vocation and fall grievously from grace.

Therefore, a priest is always aspiring to be, authentically, a living and true icon of our Lord Jesus Christ. He is called to live a continual life of repentance, mortification, sacrifice, courage, virtue, prayer, renewal. Every day. His whole life, until he finishes his earthy pilgrimage. The liturgy, with its signs and symbols, including the vesture of the priest, is a visible sign and reminder of these invisible realities. The faithful, particularly in this increasingly secular age, need to experience the sacredness of the priesthood through the sacredness of the liturgy and vice versa. It is a symbiotic relationship—the Sacred Priesthood and the Sacred Liturgy of the Church.

St. Pio of Pietrelcina, as Pope Paul VI said, was a person in his own body, but through the sacred stigmata, he was able to show, to extraordinarily manifest, the Paschal Mystery of Christ in the priesthood.

Emma de Guzman, a humble Filipino woman born on the feast of the Immaculate Conception, who is gifted in prayer and is recognized by bishops for her spiritual gifts, sees Christ in His priests. Through the La Pieta International prayer group which she founded and formed with devoted followers, she spreads her message of love, peace, and joy around the world.

Emma lives in great simplicity, traveling wherever she believes she's called to go, a true beacon in a world of spiritual darkness. I'm humbled to have served for a decade as her spiritual director while she was head of La Pieta. Although her ministry of healing and prayer is growing, Emma remains deeply humble, obedient, and always thankful to Jesus and the Blessed Mother for the blessings she has received from God. She realizes that our very lives, our salvation, depend on men anointed by God to heal, to save.

Emma Tells Her Story

Emma   Every day is a miracle for me. I always go to Church, to be with His priests, to receive Holy Communion, and to thank God that there are priests. We have to pray for priests all the time.

I became very, very spiritual from the blessings of the Lord and the Blessed Mother, all they have told me. But God gave me the chance, the gift to be with you, Fr. Machado, so that I become stronger. I learn. I become fuller in my relationship with Jesus because of you.

If you remember, we met in 1998 in Canada. I am Canadian like you. I was in Ottawa, and I invited you to come to New Jersey because we have our prayer group there. We invited prayer groups to New Jersey from Canada and the United States.

And this group invited me to go with you to the Holy Land. I was so happy! It was my first time visit to the Holy Land. It was very, very beautiful. My experience there with you and La Pieta members deepened our faith. We experienced the place of Jesus. We said, "We can die now." We can die now because we know the Bible story of Jesus.

Now we are seeing this place. Even Gethsemane, the

sorrow of our Lord, I had already experienced before in prayer. But when I went to the Holy Land, I cried, not in sorrow, in joy! My tears were full of joy because I saw in reality what happened; it was in that place.

It was beautiful. So when we were at the Church of the Beatitudes, which overlooks the Sea of Galilee, and you were celebrating the Mass, I thanked God. I thanked God we were on the top of the mountain, and I was in awe because, of course, we were in the Holy Land. You were consecrating the Host. I was looking at the Eucharist. And then I saw your face, but it was not your face—it was the face of Jesus! And the face of you, Father Machado, was not there anymore. It was the face of the *Lord*.

I was in tears. I was so quiet. Tears kept pouring and pouring out because it was such a good Lord who gave me this gift, this miracle to see the priest, to see you, Fr. Machado. We know Jesus is in the priest. Jesus is *with* the priest. He is *in* the priest. The priest is *Jesus*. When you were there on the altar, how come I saw the face of Jesus? There's only one reason.

That's why I love priests. I have respect for priests. I always say, "We have to thank God that the priests were chosen. Because without priests, we have no Eucharist of the Sacraments, which is the foundation of our Christian existence. Because the priest represents Jesus."

And we can't judge priests. We have to add them to our prayers. We cannot judge them. Whatever we do, we must understand and pray for them, because they are also human. That was what Our Lady told me in prayer: "Pray for my priests. Pray for the apostles of my Son." And the apostles I know are the bishops, the priests, the cardinals, the Holy

Father, that's what I understood, and she said, "I want you to pray for them and let my Son judge. It's between the apostles of God and my Son."

It's not for ordinary people to judge. *We have to pray.*

Photo courtesy La Pieta International Prayer Group.

*Emma with Archbishop Ramon C. Arguelles of
Lipa, the Philippines*

Window to the Holy One

So that manifestation, that miracle God showed me is so I can tell people that we need to respect our priests, "And here I AM, here I AM, at the altar, no matter what, when my priest is saying the Mass, it is me, *the Lord.*" The Lord did not tell me that, but that is what I understood.

When he is saying the Holy Mass, the priest you see on the altar, at that time you have to respect the priest. He is the window to the Holy One. What I felt there when I had that experience, that mystical experience, was that Jesus was showing me: "This is my priest and I AM, here on the altar. And I chose him to be my apostle."

In 2008, I was blessed to go to the Holy Land again. Father, you asked me to come with you and another priest.

At the Church of the Beatitudes, the same place, during Mass, I looked at you again. And I was thanking God. And here comes the Light—again! But it's not Jesus, it's bright Light. The bright Light that is Jesus' light. *I thanked God!* And then I heard this lady on the other side, the end of the row, a little bit away, it was so beautiful. This lady, Anna, I could hear her sighing loudly, and crying, but quietly. I was thinking: Maybe there's something she can feel. After the Mass, I talked to you about my experience, Father. Beautiful, again! Every time I see you, I have that manifestation, that Light. God is pleased with you.

I was telling you about my experience, that I saw a Light on the altar, and you and the other priest were covered with Light. I heard the voice of Anna. She said, "You know, I cannot understand what I see, but I could see something very strange. In my heart, I wanted to cry. There was something very, very special there on the altar." We really need priests like you, Fr. Machado, strong priests, who have no peers, to fight for our own faith. That's why Jesus showed me the beautiful light in you, around you, surrounding you, and even the priests who are with you. And the face of Jesus as you were consecrating the host.

And that's a beautiful experience. I've had it with other priests, too. I always have a very beautiful feeling, to be with those priests who are faithful to God, faithful to their vows. I can feel it.

I love priests, and I thank God that we will continue to pray for the priests here on Earth, that they will be guided by the Holy Spirit and be strong.

We will support the priests. That will be our vow, our promise as La Pieta, to help them and to make them strong, too.

I think priests should be humble also. Humility. *Humility.* Humility. If they become humble, they learn so much. We have to see priests as an instrument of God, and we have to respect priests, and know how special priests are, how beautiful. They give us blessings and help us with all our problems.

Without priests, how can we receive the Sacrament of Reconciliation? How can we be baptized?

Being priests, they have to be perfect. For years, they studied theology, the teachings of the Lord. They have to be everything they learned. And I think if they follow His teaching, there will be beautiful relationships between people and priests. If this priest is holy, he's not just an ordinary person; he is a special gift of God for us, ordained to the Church. We need priests in this time of depression.

The world, the spirituality of the people, it's not there anymore. We have to pray for people to be strong in their Faith, too.

St. John: Behold Thy Sons

When in prayer I spoke with St. John the Apostle, he, too, talked about priests. He said: *"Love! Love! Love your priests."* It's all love.

He talked about how priests should have the same mind and heart, the love, the love of God. *The same heart!* He said, "I am an apostle of God," and he was asking that all priests have that same heart and same mind and that love faithful to God, like St. John. So many things are happening now, the persecution of priests, and that's why now we need to pray for priests. And appreciate that we have priests. We have to love priests and support them. And respect them.

In the Philippines, Fr. Machado, I know you are always happy to meet my countrymen. Why? When we see priests, we're always are on our knees. We kiss the hands of the priest. We always have respect, because we were brought up like that.

Priests are chosen to help us, to bless us. I cannot bless myself. You're the one who'll bless me and you will give me absolution when I ask for forgiveness. You are the one who will bless and forgive us before God, because God is inside you.

Kindly do your ministry as a priest and think of Jesus beside you. He is *beside* you!"

We need priests now because there aren't many young people who enter an order to be a priest. How many people do we have to help them and support them? Because it's true: One day we'll have no more priests. I feel that.

Years will come where there are more persecutions of priests. That's why we need to help you, Father, in prayers, to pray for priests, for more priests, that they will be strong. To defend our Faith and to defend priests.

In La Pieta, as children of God, we try to be faithful to God and we are happy. We thank you, Father, for elevating us and directing us to God.

I know God is always with us. I know that He will never, never leave us. I know He loves His priests. And He knows also His priests are weak. And He wants us to pray for them. There will be good relationships *because of our faith*. And when we believe that priests are sent by God, there will be peace, love, joy in this world. ~🝱

✝

Prayer for Your Priest as He Prepares for Holy Mass

Oh Lord Jesus Christ, in the celebration of the Holy Sacrifice of the Mass, you are Priest, Altar, and Victim. I pray that the priest celebrant, as he prepares to offer up the Holy Sacrifice of Calvary, may do so with unsullied hands, a pure intention, a righteous heart, a clear conscience, and integral devotion. May he be a living oblation of total love to the Father for the praise and the glory of His name, for our good, and the good of all His Church. *Through Jesus Christ, Our Lord,* **Amen.**

Prayer for the Spiritual Perfection of Priests

Oh Lord, you call your chosen to be perfect as your heavenly Father is perfect. May our beloved priests aspire to the greatest heights of perfection in holiness. Although they may be vessels of clay, you imbue them with the greatest spiritual treasures. They are channels and privileged instruments of sanctification for all the faithful. May they be renewed and fortified in the gift and mystery of your priesthood so as to radiate your divine perfections. *Through Jesus Christ, Our Lord,* **Amen.**

"For if this most holy sacrament were only celebrated in one place, and consecrated by only one priest in the world, how great a desire would men have to go to that place, and to such a priest of God; that they might see the divine mysteries celebrated?"

~ **Thomas à Kempis,**
Imitation of Christ

Sacramental Friendship
Chapter 8

Our struggle as priests is the mystery of the Cross. Its contradictions. Its frustrations. Its pain.

Each day, the Catholic priest puts on the living yoke of his holy calling: the Roman collar of obedience whose white hints at eternity, and with his cassock, the sash of chastity, the color black for simplicity and penance. For he, a priest, is dying to self so that he can rise to serve the Lord, to witness the Kingdom to Come.

He is ... he wears ... he lives ... the Church's signs and language.

Blessed Columba Marmion in his classical work, *Christ, The Ideal of the Priest* (© 2005, Ignatius Press), wrote that the sacrament of Holy Orders was instituted to confer on men the power to consecrate the Body and Blood of Christ. "The purpose of the imposition of hands is the communication of this power. When the priest celebrates the *mysterium fidei,* he is not merely carrying out one of the many functions attached to the high dignity of his state; he is accomplishing the one essential act of that state. This act involves an exercise of power far above that required for any other exercise of his ministry either ritual or pastoral. That is why the whole life of the priest should be an echo or a prolongation of his Mass."

A *prolongation* of his Mass. Something infinitely greater than nuclear fission or combustion in the created universe, a divine energy radiated throughout the world. *A fire!* From a man ordained by God, who brings his love, his life, his poverty of spirit, to be kindled in the fiery passion of Jesus' Sacred Heart. *Behold the Man!* Behold the humanity cloaked by the divinity who is Christ; behold the humanity of the priest that cloaks his supernatural gifts and mission.

Even in poverty, the priest is the richest man in the world. For his love seeks heaven's treasure. Each day he consecrates the Blessed Sacrament of the Altar, worth more than all the trillions of dollars in the world, more than all the gold and diamond mines beneath the Earth. The CEO extraordinaire, you might say, in the business vernacular that seems to captivate our world.

In the canonization process for Mother Teresa— it's amazing how quickly she was beatified—they compiled several hundred volumes, details of hundreds of miracles, connected to the Blessed Mother of Calcutta. The difference between saints like Mother Teresa and us is that we take too much for granted. Christ comes to us every day, through His priests, and yet what do we do? Do we recognize the day of the Lord?

Mother Teresa, when she walked past the Blessed Sacrament, wouldn't just *stroll* by, she would *profoundly bow* or *genuflect*. Right away she was there, with Our Lord, Jesus Christ.

It gave me shudders once when she pointed to the tabernacle and asked: "How is it possible, this miracle of God?" And she took my hands and said, "These hands hold the greatest treasure, far beyond what the universe can contain." She had such reverence for the Holy Hands of a priest that she bent down to kiss my hands, and looking at me with those eyes, the eyes of Blessed Mother Teresa, she said, "Father, never, ever forget. I am not just kissing *your* hands, I am kissing the hands of *Our Lord, Jesus Christ!*"

More Than the World Contains

Without the priest, we wouldn't have this treasure on the altar, or in the tabernacle. But until we understand this, we'll have no gratitude.

The anointed hands, consecrated for the Blessed Sacrament of the Altar, the hands that bless, that absolve, the hands of the priesthood, those are hands belonging to a man with the greatest vocation, the most sublime vocation, because as priest, he represents Jesus Christ.

St. John Mary Vianney, in his *Little Catechism of the Curé of Ars,* (© 1951, TAN Books) says, "If I were to meet a priest and an angel, I should salute the priest before I saluted the angel. The latter is a friend of God; but the priest holds His place.

"When you see a priest, you should say, 'There is he who made me a child of God, and opened Heaven to me by holy Baptism; he who purified me after I had sinned; who gives nourishment to my soul.'" When I hold the Blessed Sacrament as He did, I look upon more than anything the world contains.

Sometimes when I am celebrating Holy Mass, I get lost in that gaze, looking upon the face of our Lord and Savior. The Sacred Host, the Blessed Sacrament—what more could anyone want? *"Seek ye the face of Jesus, and He will provide unto thee."* No questions asked. *"Seek the Kingdom of Heaven and all these things will be added unto thee."*

What's unclear?

People say they want vocations, but they take priests for granted. Those who have a father or grandmother who fosters love and respect for the priesthood, or who rises regularly in the middle of the night to pray, as my grandmother did, know there are profound blessings upon them, a generational blessing. God doesn't call an individual to the priesthood out of a vacuum. He prepares a family as a seeding ground. It may take one or two generations. That's how fragile the seed of vocation is in the priesthood and religious life.

In a special *Year for Priests,* we supported, prayed for, and sustained the priesthood by empathizing with the struggles and challenges each priest faces. Through prayer and sacrifice we prayed for the rehabilitation and renewal of priests who had struggled and fallen or not lived up to the grace and state of their vocation. We priests, together with our Holy Father, together with Christ's faithful, proclaimed with wonder and awe the great beauty of Christ's love in the priesthood.

Having had the chance as a deacon to assist the now Venerable Pope John Paul II in the Holy Sacrifice of the

Mass and to celebrate a few years later as a priest a more private service, I always was inspired by the Holy Father's eminently priestly example. In my life, he has been the greatest model of living the priestly mystery of Christ, with great dignity, courage, faith, reverence, and divine charity. Celebrating with the Holy Father was an experience of *wonder*. It was a celebration of the Heavenly Liturgy, the Divine Liturgy. As a priest, I could identify with Christ the Priest, as lived out and exemplified by the person and ministry of Pope John Paul II.

The priesthood also has a profound friendship, with Christ and with the greatest brotherhood in the world. The sacramental brotherhood is intricately linked with the Sacrament of Holy Orders and the episcopacy. Sacramentally, we become collaborators with the bishop in the mission of the Church. So the bishop becomes a spiritual, sacramental father to the presbyteral brethren. He's the moderator and promoter *par excellence* in his diocese of this priestly assembly. To the extent the bishop encourages and strengthens priests' spiritual and supernatural brotherhood, the more effective will be the bishop's apostolic work.

When I met Fr. Walter, an Australian priest, in 1997, I learned he'd been ordained in his late 40s. After his ordination, he was told, "Welcome to the Catholic priesthood, the world's greatest brotherhood."

Unfortunately, that's not the case today. It seems to me that each priest works in isolation, particularly on the diocesan level, each man to himself. Deanery meetings and gatherings offer opportunities for brotherhood. But there appears to be a crisis of the priesthood, in its supernatural understanding of the brotherhood. What priests need to understand is that their brotherhood is a human brother-hood whose interaction is based on a supernatural reality. It's not a blood brotherhood, or one with ethnic bonds. The supernatural call unites priests from different backgrounds and tongues. It's Christ the High Priest who's father and brother. Christ the High Priest has a paternal role in reflect-ing God the Father's love for His Son. God the Father has the primary role. I'm not saying Christ primarily reflects the role of brother. He's brother and friend to His priests.

Remember Christ's words in the gospel of St. John, at the Last Supper? *"No do not call you servants any longer, because the servant does not know what the master is doing; but I have called you friends, because I have made known to you everything that I have heard from my Father"* (John 15:15).

Although we're still the Lord's servants, we serve Him out of intimate friendship with Christ. And we're not mere functionaries. Just as Christ came down and suffered for us, so too do we emphasize suffering, and support for the people of God.

One way we support the people is by the example we priests set as we relate to one another. For example, in a local church where priests exhibit great charity and love and support one another in faithful obedience to their superiors, and the diocesan bishop, and the Holy Father—those priests will generate great conversions. They'll be a tremendous source of apostolic zeal and fruitfulness. They'll be a source of abundant sanctification.

But it's not a question of just having an affinity with one or another priest. Otherwise we'd degenerate into priestly cliques. We should see the face of Christ, the face of our own priesthood, in our fellow priest, even if he comes from a different background, or if we don't have a natural affinity toward each other.

The brotherhood of priests should be through one mind and one heart with the Church—*Sentire Cum Ecclesia*—a termed coined by St. Ignatius, "to think with the Church," the Mystical Bride and Body of Christ. There should be a loving submission, to the will and intellect of the teachings of Christ and articulated by the language of the Church. There should be submission to the Magesterium, and loving obedience to the Holy Father and the diocesan bishop. And for priests who belong to communities, loving obedience to their superiors, too.

Therefore there's unity of the brotherhood itself with the Church hierarchy and the rest of the faithful of Christ. It's a unity characterized by the supernatural and morally infused virtues, particularly the theological virtues of Faith, Hope, and Love. If a brother priest cannot see or serve Christ in another brother priest, how can he serve or see Christ in the faithful, let alone the poor or non-Christian or nonbeliever?

Called Out of Darkness

A priest enters and leads spiritual combat in Christian life. "The great figures of prayer of the Old Covenant before Christ, as well as the Mother of God, the saints, and he himself, all teach us this: Prayer is a battle. Against whom? Against ourselves and against the wiles of the tempter who does all he can to turn man away from prayer, away from union with God. We pray as we live, because we live as we pray. If we do not want to act habitually according to the Spirit of Christ, neither can we pray habitually in His name. The 'spiritual battle' of the Christian's new life is inseparable from the battle of prayer" *(Catechism of the Catholic Church, 2725).*

The priest is at the forefront of this combat between Christ and Satan, grace and sin, virtue and vice. There's a battle to overcome and prevail against the world, the flesh, and the devil. The Church's great mystics and spiritual authors framed the battle in similar terms.

Recall how St. Paul, as related in his second letter to the Corinthians, asked the Lord to remove the thorn of a demonic agent: *"Therefore, to keep me from being too elated, a thorn was given to me in the flesh, a messenger of Satan to torment me, to keep me from being too elated. Three times I appealed to the Lord about this, that it would leave me, but He said to me, 'My grace is sufficient for you, for [my] power is made perfect in weakness'" (2 Cor. 12 7-9).*

The priest is purified and fortified, strengthened through the trials and sufferings of his life. He is purified from attachment to sin, the uprooting of vice, the reparation of sin, and eventually overcoming the devil by making up in his own body what is lacking in the sufferings of Christ.

So the priest becomes a true icon of the Crucified One. He lives the depths of the Paschal Mystery of the Lord's Passion, Suffering and Death and the triumph of His Resurrection.

The priest continuously lives the Paschal Mystery through his lifelong sufferings and struggles. He is one with Christ on the Cross in the celebration of the Eucharist. He is one with Christ—Priest, Altar, and Victim—who offers himself up to the Father for our salvation and redemption.

However, the pain of Good Friday, the tragedy of Good Friday and apparent scandal of the Cross, gives way to joy and hope with the Resurrection of Easter Sunday. From darkness, we pass into light. I always loved that sentence in the first Eucharist Prayer, from 1 Peter 2:9: *"Everywhere we proclaim your mighty works for you have called us out of darkness into your own wonderful light."* In the lives of St. Pio and other priests, we see the passion and suffering of Christ, lived in an extraordinary manner, supernatural manifestations of the sacred stigmata. We share the miraculous wounds as a reminder of our Lord's Passion.

But the priest's suffering is not an end in itself, but a means to an end, just as Good Friday is, leading to the joy of Easter Sunday. Therefore, we're called to live out the Paschal Mystery in its totality. We become a living Holy Week Tridiuum, mystically.

The priest is at the forefront of the Church's mission, as Christ is at the forefront of the Gospel, subjected to and targeted by temptations and attacks, spiritual and even physical attacks. However, we enjoy, as our Lord said to St. Paul, special blessings, spiritual graces, and charisms that enable us to fend off these attacks. And not just survive, but thrive, spiritually. And to achieve great sanctity—for ourselves, and for the flock entrusted to our care.

Our Eucharistic Hearts

A colleague priest, Fr. Michael Tapajna of the Missionaries of the Most Blessed Sacrament, also has a worldwide mission. He travels, preaching the word of God to the English-speaking of the world, to help establish Blessed Sacrament chapels in parishes everywhere. He's experiencing in his ministry an unprecedented renaissance in Eucharistic devotion and in conversation will always note that "literally at this hour, tens of thousands of people are praying in a chapel before the Blessed Sacrament." Imagine the graces dispensed from the open heart of Our Lord!

At Our Father's Chapel at St. Dunstan's Cathedral Basilica in Prince Edward Island in Canada, for instance, as many as 10 people each hour adore the Eucharistic Lord. It's unprecedented, Fr. Tapajna says, in that never before have there been so many people concentrated, praying before the Blessed Sacrament.

Years ago, Eucharistic Adoration typically occurred in convents or in monasteries, but there were exceptions to that rule. Most Adoration was driven by religious. In the Middle Ages, hermits prayed before the Blessed Sacrament, and for many monks, it was tradition that they have the Blessed Sacrament in their cells.

But as a result of the movement of the Holy Spirit in the last 25 or 30 years, there are many more laity praying every day and night before the Blessed Sacrament, Fr. Tapajna says. The Real Presence Eucharistic Education and Adoration Association says there are more than 7,000 exposition sites in the United States alone, about 1,000 of them perpetual Adoration, the rest with Adoration suspended for weekend Masses or at nighttime.

Together with the U.S. chapels, there are thousands of perpetual Adoration chapels worldwide, like that at the Basilique du Sacré-Coeur on France's Montmartre, the highest point in Paris, where the Lord has been praised and adored for more than 100 years. "So we've gone from almost no parish-driven chapels—that is lay-driven chapels—to thousands worldwide,"

Fr. Tapajna says. "How profound the movement has been—I've helped open 200 chapels—it really does show a powerful movement of the Holy Spirit."

He says it is holy inspiration and witness like that of a small parish in Arkansas, with 500 parishioners, that has prompted other parishes to do the same. That parish has sustained perpetual Eucharistic Adoration for 10 years.

Fr. Tapajna says great fruit has come of this mission, including healings, conversions, and vocations. "A woman I know, her conversion came about when someone introduced her to an Adoration chapel," he says. "She was a Baptist and she found tremendous peace going into a small room to pray. The moment the woman walked into the room where Jesus was exposed in the Blessed Sacrament, it was 'game over.' And she didn't even know what the Eucharist is." The experience led her return to the Catholic Church.

"Another lady, known as a 'New Age Queen,' someone far gone into that movement, who had studied New Age teachings for years and years, then was teaching others, somehow by the grace of God, I was able to suggest he come with me to Eucharistic Adoration, even for five minutes. The reaction she had the moment she walked into the Presence of Our Lord, when she saw His Presence, she began to weep and sob. She was 100 percent aware of the Almighty. She dropped it all—10 years of study. Now she spends all the time she can before the Blessed Sacrament."

Jesus told St. Margaret Mary in revelation before the Blessed Sacrament that if more people came to Him in this august sacrament, as He saw an increase in devotion and gratitude to His Sacred Presence, there would be an outpouring of the Holy Spirit, blessings as never before.

"One of the things I find fascinating about that revelation," Fr. Tapajna says, "is that Jesus said he was deeply hurt by the coldness, indifference, and ingratitude, particularly of the elect, to His Real Presence in this Sacrament. And then He reveals that He would pour out a staggering amount of grace if people come to Him."

Fr. Tapajna says in the Cayman Islands, a British protectorate that is largely Protestant, there's a Eucharistic Adoration chapel at St. Ignatius Parish that's been operating for nearly 10 years.

One parishioner has become interested in the permanent deaconate, and a family on the island all three children, are discerning vocations to the religious life.

"I love it when someone far from the Lord or a Protestant who often doesn't even understand what the Eucharist is, has an experience. I'm always stunned by their description. They see this gold object [the monstrance] on a table. And so very often, they speak in poetic and passionate terms when they walk into this room, as opposed to any room beside it. They speak of peace, the likes of which they've never experienced. ... there's such a hunger to be genuinely healed, to be touched by the Divine Physician."

I experience this in my own ministry. The Divine Physician often says "game over." And in the story that Fr. Dan Havron tells, through the movement of grace, the sacraments, throughout Holy Scripture, and the invisible yet tangible movement of the Holy Spirit, God can draw good, can heal, can use illness and difficulty to make you holy, to develop and form your character. We're the clay; the Lord is the master potter.

The story my brother in Christ Fr. Dan shares is a testament to the profound faith of a priest living fully in the person of his priesthood, who recognizes his dignity in the humanity and divinity of Jesus Christ. Fr. Dan has not only faith in his own healing gifts, through Christ but also a deep love for the Eucharistic Lord and for his brother priests.

But his ministry goes far beyond one experience of Jesus passing by. It's grounded in his deep devotion, his vocation, and service to our Lord and Savior, Jesus Christ. He realizes his sacred dignity and honors the character of the priesthood, which bears a mark upon the clay of his soul. He lives the brotherhood of Christ, His fatherhood, and divine Sonship. By Baptism, he is a Child of God, yet a priest whose faith and action is supremely guided by the core of his being: *He lives a prolongation of his Mass.*

Fr. Dan Tells His Story

My ministry as a Franciscan priest is preaching and teaching the word of God and the Gospel of Life, the renewal of lay people through the Catholic Church. I had been a high school teacher from the time of my ordination on June 11, 1977, to May 1985, teaching religion and journalism.

I was very taken by my ministry. We did a lot of praying over people for inner and physical healing, and I had paid much attention to that. My grandmother was an advocate of Our Lady of Lourdes. I was eight years old when I saw her leave her home to fly to France, for the 100th

Anniversary of Lourdes, and here we are just completing the celebration of the 150th anniversary of the apparitions. I still remember 50 years ago so clearly. She would tell me about healing miracles. I was raised on that kind of faith: *The Lord can do anything. And healing is an integral part of believing.* It was tucked away in the seeds of my faith life.

In 1985, my provincial requested that I move from the high school in Fort Wayne, Ind., to the School of Evangelization in Detroit to head the inner healing ministry. I got involved with faith-filled people, charismatic renewal, and we were trying to draw as many Catholics as possible, learning about adult commitment and renewal of their faith. I would see 500 people a week for classes, healing services, Confessions, retreats—we had everything. I didn't know much about healing, but I believed in it.

I ended up undergoing a profound reawakening in my faith. There were wonderful people on staff. We prayed every day as a staff.

We decided together what we would teach for courses every semester, waiting on the Lord's inspiration. All of the work depended on a move of the Lord's hand. We listened for the Lord as a staff and then interpreted messages received as a staff. There were seven or eight of us. Fr. Duane Stenzel, O.F.M., priest-director at *Radio Maria,* in Alexandria, La., was my priest and retreat mentor. He gave me a profound conviction that Jesus Christ would do anything in this world to move hearts. It was a wonderful and exciting seven to eight years in my ministry.

After that, I was transferred to downtown Detroit and became pastor of an inner city parish, with a Carmelite sister on staff, and was evangelization director for the Diocese of

Detroit—five counties, 320 parishes—all under the oversight of Adam Cardinal Maida.

From reading about people like St. Bernadine of Siena, a 15th century Franciscan preacher who lived through the reign of 11 popes, I learned that people would change if priests got on fire with trust. God would move them. It's a frightening thing when you preach to people and He tells them to move.

While I was preaching at Mass one Sunday, a woman yelled out: "Fr. Dan! I believe you can heal this arm of mine!" This was in the summer of '92. The woman had been attacked on the street. Someone tried to take her pocketbook, but it was wrapped around her wrist, so it cracked her wrist, and the wrist was horribly swollen. "This priest up here is going to heal me!" she exclaimed to the church. "He's going to heal you *all!*" She stepped out in faith, and came right up front. "I said, I want you to heal me right now," she demanded, in faith. A couple of people from the pews came up and prayed with us, and instantly, the wrist was whole. The swelling went down.

Another time I was dining with an Iraqi family, and the grandmother had horrible carpal tunnel syndrome. During the blessing of the meal, I prayed for healing over her wrist. And during the meal, the father of the home said, "I did not believe this stuff was true, or why others believe God can work holy miracles." So I stepped out in faith—we should not question what God can do—and I asked the grandmother to put her wrist up and show what God *can* do. She lifted her hand, and it was perfectly restored.

I was healed after a car wreck. I had neuropathy and sciatica, and it was going on for weeks. Someone gave me a medallion of Ven. Fr. Solanus Casey, the Capuchin Franciscan whose cause for canonization is under way. It contained a relic of his habit. I was told to put it in my waistband. I did. After weeks of struggling, every single bit of pain was gone.

I began to witness a lot of healing. I got to expect miraculous healing all the time. Our experiences lead us forward in our faith life.

I remember other healings, too, like the time in 1985 at the friary where I lived in Detroit when a mother with a daughter who was an ice skater, maybe 11-12 years old, came right into the dining room. The girl had fallen on the ice for a third time. It was her third fracture, and she was in a cast. The mother said, "I need some friars to pray over my daughter. I believe she can be healed." Three of us prayed over her. The mother found out at the next X-ray that not only was the fracture gone; there was no scar tissue from the other two fractures. Everything was completely and totally restored.

Great, great miracles.

Another time, in 1987, I was holding a retreat for high school juniors, with a Vietnam vet. He was Pentecostal, but really Catholic in his heart. He and I and another Franciscan were speaking to the juniors in the high school. The cafeteria was packed. This vet told about life on the front lines, and talked about growing up with Christ and making a strong commitment in our lives. And it was part of the retreat day to pray over everyone. It happened to be in the fall when the kids were active in sports so some were walking with crutches, others had wrists in casts, and we prayed over all of them for healing. And every one of them was healed. Right there. They couldn't contain these five or six kids who were healed. The other kids were watching. These kids, they were all running and jumping.

The next day was the retreat for the high school seniors. I haven't thought about this for a long time—the awesome glory and power of God!—and the next day ... we came up to the school ... and they were beating down the doors to get into the cafeteria. *Beating down the doors.* More kids were healed that day. They were—it was like a mob. We never met these kids before. We'd been invited by the school chaplain. The senior boys were rushing to get seats in the front, and I said to the Vietnam Veteran, Larry: "How do we top yesterday?" He said he had been praying about it: "We're going to get them to pray over each other and they'll all be healed, too."

That's what we did. And the same thing happened.

You couldn't contain them.

The Path to Inner Healing

I think people are getting sick and tired of being cultural pagans. They see in the Catholic Church that deadwood can disappear like melting ice. But it takes people motivated by the Spirit of Fire to do it. It is the Holy Spirit. You have to believe in the Lord. And trust in anything.

As a Franciscan, I was trained in the mid-1970s, when all of us were following the Church the best we knew. There was great experimentation in everything and oftentimes a lack of clarity. But my sense of the priesthood began to change with Pope John Paul II. There was greater clarity and greater direction. I began to see the first element in two areas: More intensive prayer, and being in a community of people living a deep and profound faith in God in the modern age. People lived with the expectation that God works wonders in people's lives. If we have faith, people convert and live lives for God. It taught me about holiness, that we are all called to a radical shift through conversion, to not just being busy people, but to take time to pray; to surrender our entire life to our Lord Jesus Christ; and to put our conversation, our family life, all, under His authority.

I learned about obedience, ongoing conversion, daily prayer, work, and the voice of the Holy Spirit in my life. I learned to have a greater and deeper faith in the manifestation of God in my ministry. I'd give all my challenges in ministry to God, pray, and expect the Lord to work wonders. And many times He would. At the School of Evangelization, miracles, deliverance, great conversions were all common occurrences.

I experienced inner healing—wonderful healing and some deeply felt hurts and angers. This changed my self-concept and my self-confidence.

The people who ministered to me in mid 1980s got in touch with that and formed me in prayer, and my life changed profoundly.

And then the inner person within me needed to understand the new man in Christ Jesus and die to my old self. I have always sensed a rebirth into humility and in that Christ Jesus moves me profoundly, as I place all things in Him. I still feel a constant newness and rejuvenation in Christ all the time. I'm turning 59, and my hair is grayer, but

I don't have a sense of aging or burning out or bad health—nothing is a setback.

"I am the light of the world. Whoever follows me will never walk in darkness but will have the light of life" (John 8:12). I use this Scriptural passage in personal prayer and in spiritual direction. The basic dynamic is not to look at the darkness around us, but to look to Christ. We are being transformed always in the Lord. St. Paul says, "No longer is it I who live, but Christ Jesus who lives in me." He transforms and recircuits anything within us, for healing and renewal and rejuvenation—a new life.

That's where I've come from. When I preach and teach, I do it with deep conviction, with all things given over to the Holy Spirit. I stand within Christ Jesus and He within me when I speak to the people of God. Jesus gives me a sense of responsibility and enjoyment in what I'm doing. The Lord gives me the disposition, and what I need to have when I'm preaching to a congregation. You know when you're doing what He's called you to do, because your words are effective and carry the anointing of the Holy Spirit. You can see it in the eyes of the people sitting before you.

Our Spirits Connect

I met you, Fr. Machado, when I was stationed at the St. Francis Retreat House in Easton, Pa. I felt a deep connection in my spirit, because I sensed you experienced your ministry much like mine. You were forthright, especially when it came to deliverance and exorcism; I was quieter about it when I taught and preached. You have, for me, been an inspiration as far as boldness of the Gospel, preaching in season and out of season, and not reneging on all that the Gospel of Life demands.

You, Father, always have a wonderful sense of paternity with priests. I feel like your brother when I am with you. You respect. You listen. This is whether I am with you 20 minutes, a half hour, an hour. Even in an off-the-cuff situation, it's always Christ-centered: What's the next strategy for the people of God? Where's the next retreat? How is the Spirit moving? What miracles have you heard of? It's all very encouraging. You give witness to the hand of God, and give fire to the witness of God in the world.

You were one of the first priests I experienced who, not only in Adoration but also in times of prayer, carried the monstrance and placed the Eucharistic Lord on sick people's bodies, their heads or shoulders. You also bless with the Eucharistic Lord at the end of Benediction or after the short deliverance prayer.

The last time you were on retreat, your voice emitted such volume that the first three pews of people jumped in the air! One woman fell on the floor. And someone screamed out loud. It was a physical lifting of the powers of darkness. People were physically lifted.

People come to me after you've long gone, and tell me about healings they received or inner healing. You have a way in Confession of being extremely prophetic in people's lives. The amount of time and energy you invest in souls has born great fruit. Some people are in tears when they leave Confession, and are so upset at your insistence that they go back and deal with this issue in their lives. You're not afraid to challenge them. I was moved during one of your talks, when you said that the day I begin to co-opt the world's values, I can't stand in front of God's people to preach prophetic messages—that's the day I lose the privilege of the priesthood, and the power of the prophetic word.

Fraternity of the Priesthood

People need to know that our vocation is calling us to give authentic life witness. People think of the priesthood standing in the person of Jesus, in terms of consecrating, ritualizing the sacraments, but do people think even more than that, or more broadly than that? That the priest is called to a prophetic place in how he acts and what he does; in the person he is? The prophetic dimension is essential. You, Father, believe that deeply, and you call people to that. You get fired up around priests who feel that way. You want to call priests who are more convicted in the life of the Church.

Within you, you have a sense of brotherhood, a fraternity in the priesthood, with other priests. You openly share about the Church, how the Church is struggling. You see people really moving ahead and others who just don't care. And that affects you. I know it does, when it comes to the whole human side to being a priest. It's draining for you, and all of us, to minister and be present to people. But we do it. Christ did, so we must.

Father, I know how busy you are, *but you always take time.* Like the night we sat, 10 p.m. until midnight, two hours on a Friday, eating cantaloupe in the basement kit-chen, drinking water, praying together. ... I always feel like you bring me through, by your very sense of compassion and care, you bring me through to a place where I have a profound sense for my own dignity and respect for myself. That's a real part of the healing. And that's not necessarily the intention of what you've come for, but it's the byproduct of how you see yourself or how I see a priest's presence. It's the *incarnational* way of how Christ was a man with other men and women. It's the element of care. And friendship. And compassion. Just being *human*. It sends off such healing and affirmation to people.

Christ Jesus in the moment of Incarnation, in the womb of his mother—St. Louis de Montfort experienced this in private revelation and said—His first emotion had to be ecstasy.

You have an amazing sense as a priest, Father, of the depth of what it means to know Christ. It's not quote-unquote, "He lives in me." It's "How did He live in the womb of His mother? What were His experiences? How did He feel?" You call people to be sensitive, to take time to ponder the depths of Christ's humanity in a womb of a woman touched by the Holy Spirit.

Praying, and praying with you, made me more sensitive to the things I teach. It's easy for us not to be influenced by our own words, the ways in which we minister and preach. Even the things I pray for and give through my hands, I ask: Let me be touched by them as I minister to others. We stand *in persona Christi,* so Jesus is teaching us, preaching to us, even as we minister! It's powerful.

And that is my experience with you, Father, being with you. You raise the subject and integrate it. So being a priest among people heightens the sense of the Spirit and that brings an experience of faith—and keeps it alive. You know how we are: We take so much in all the time, it can go in one ear and out the other and we tend to lose it.

It's amazing what deliverance prayers do for us. They take the jaded spirit within, and help us to realize what *is* supernatural. We can become so insensitive to the supernatural. The prayers revive the child within us, as though we see things for the first time.

Being with you, sitting and talking one evening, I honest-to-God experienced not only an anointing coming from you but also an inner healing around the things we talked about. You communicated the Holy Spirit, and therefore communicated healing. *The shadow of St. Peter (Acts 5:15)*—I experienced that with you. *An anointing.* A sense of God's closeness. Holiness of God. The presence of the Holy Spirit. A sense of the Holy Spirit's reverence.

I also am taken aback by how firm you can be with people. You're not interested in making friends with the world. You cut to the chase, whether it be in Holy Confession, counseling, one-on-one sharing, or spiritual direction outside of Confession. The Spirit works through you in admonition, in exhorting others to change. And we do.

I felt in a way you were calling me to *more* in my ministry, something greater. I felt at one with you and encouraged. I felt affirmed and called forth.

At some time I have to abandon so much of my need for security and step out into the unknown. Isn't that what Jesus did with people? They had secure occupations as fishermen and now he called them into a new life.

The Lord is calling us to a clear pathway for a deeper and bolder committed life. How far am I going to let the Lord lead me? My experience of you, Father, has been to be bold and trust what God can do, in healing. In relationship with the Lord, the Lord will never abandon us, even through His Cross. So where does the healing take me? And who is there to call me to something deeper?

Hopefully, it's the priest.

The Secret of Time

Finally, I must tell of my personal experience through your healing prayer.

In early fall 2007, you were at the Retreat House. I had noticed this strange growth under the skin. I wasn't sure how deep it ran. I could see and feel it, a bump on my throat. I could put my fingers around it, like a framing nail sitting under the skin, maybe 3½ inches long. I went to a general practitioner, and he had a clinic with two other MD's. He couldn't figure it out, although he didn't think it was inside the carotid artery. Neither of his colleagues could figure it out. He wanted me to get a CT scan, to see how deep it was.

The secret of time happened.

It was with me about two weeks. I scheduled the CT scan the Monday after your retreat. On Sunday afternoon, at the healing service, I asked you to pray over it. You took the Blessed Sacrament from the altar, and asked everyone to pray for me. You placed the monstrance on my throat and on my head. You were pushing with all your might, so much so I was pushed over, leaning. You prayed for a moment or so. I was just thinking in confidence: *The Lord is going to heal me*. I trusted your prayer and the power of the Lord. I told the Lord if he wanted one more "gimped-up" priest, He'd have him on hand, but if I could keep my health, I would go to the ends of the Earth for Him. The next day, I went for the CT scan, and it was all gone. They found nothing; I was as clean as a whistle. The report came back and said nothing was there. The nurse, she didn't know what she was doing the CT scan for. I showed her: "This is where it was supposed to be." But the test showed nothing.

On parish missions and retreats, many people get prayed over. And people just come to life again. When I've prayed over people, I see the Blessed Mother, the Sacred Heart of Jesus, Padre Pio, the visitation of the Angels.

The Blessed Mother cares about us, her children! She is amazing. She has a mantle she wraps around people that I see all the time.

The Holy Spirit comes in golden colors of lights, showering people, anointing them, healing them. It's always an amazing thing to watch. I see them around people and I pray. *I can't believe how real and present God is to them.* It is a great blessing. Faith builds up and builds up.

Fr. Thomas Acklin, O.S.B., wrote a wonderful book, *The Unchanging Heart of the Priesthood, (© 2005, Emmaus Road Publishing)* and you, Father Machado, remind me of what he speaks: "The priest then is not a 'substitute' or a stand-in for Christ like a proxy at a meeting. Or a substitute teacher in a grade school. The priest makes Christ the Shepherd present in a way similar to the way that Eucharistic Bread is not just a 'sign' that Christ is present but rather the sacrament of the Eucharist makes Him present in a special way." You, Father, make the priesthood come to life in me; the impact of the priesthood in my own life that I didn't experience before. Real, personal, impact. Fr. Acklin says the person of the priest is supposed to be consumed, used up, in service and dedication and humiliation, heightened in the promises Christ gives to us as we spend ourselves for Him, remembering His Passion and Death and Resurrection.

My sense is that Pope Benedict, in a *Year for Priests,* called all of us back to our true identity. What is that? Jesus is calling people to conversion. I think what the Holy Father did was to call us to holiness—not just to a lot of work. Ministry as an expression of the priesthood. Americans like to work if they're healthy enough. It gives us meaning. But when we derive meaning from work and not holiness, our ontological nature gets lost. The very holiness of God has changed our very nature. That's a direct gift from Christ in the mystery of the Incarnation.

Fr. Acklin, citing John 10:36, wrote that Christ refers to Himself as from the Father, as consecrated and sent into the world. What he means is we are consecrated through our Baptism, and as a priest that's what it means to be consecrated by our Father in Christ Jesus. Christ refers to a personal consecration and therefore is sent into the world. Our ministry flows from our personal consecration. If I do not have a sense of holiness, the very nature of who I am, then I miss the point altogether, and I become a robot.

It's *personal consecration.* And this personal consecration is like Christ Jesus sent into the world. When we forget who we are and can be, or only pay attention to part of that, we're working in a bipolar way. And only part of our self is engaged. We don't have the full man living or working or being aware of whom we truly are. *We're consecrated beings sent into the world.* Pope Benedict XVI called us to greater holiness, to a greater sense of the fullness of the priesthood.

A greater sense of *who we are.* ~

✝

Prayer for the Unity of the Priesthood

Lord, Jesus Christ, as Supreme High Priest, you called the Apostles and their successors into communion and sacramental friendship. Your priests, as collaborators of the Bishops, are called into the sacred bonds of friendship through the order of the presbyterate. We pray that all priests may grow in loving unity through You. *Through Jesus Christ, Our Lord,* **Amen.**

Prayer for Priestly Vocations

Oh Lord, from the beginning of time you called men to serve as priests of your dearly beloved Son, Our Lord, Jesus Christ. May we beg you to send more workers into your Vineyard, for the harvest is plentiful but the laborers are few. Therefore, we raise our hearts and voices, oh Lord of the Harvest, asking you to shower a broken world in need of conversion and sanctification with an abundance of priestly vocations. *Through Jesus Christ, Our Lord,* **Amen.**

"Do not abandon yourselves to despair. We are the Easter people and hallelujah is our song."
                                        ~ Pope John Paul II

Epilogue
Salt of the Earth

C hrist's priests need people to support them—not as "consumers" of the priesthood, but as the salt of the Earth—loving, prayerful devotees of this great ministry. After all, we all have a role in the plan of salvation.

I think of two families, who, among many others, have had a significant impact in my ministry. But above all, I've marveled at the great supernatural love they have for each and every priest they meet. I'm thinking of Paul and Ellen Zsebedics, and their family, of Gaithersburg, Md., and Fred and Leslie Dupy, and their family, in Springfield, Mo.

Fred and Paul are both successful businessmen, family men, and men devoted to Christ. Fred, raised as a Southern Baptist, is now Catholic, and loves the priesthood. If you ask him, he'll tell you how a blessing from a priest saved his family's 1,040-acre Oklahoma farm from drought and damaging hail. More dramatically, he'll share how a blessing saved his business from fire. Listen to his witness, his pro-clamation, his *kerygma:*

"About six months after you blessed the business, in 2007, Father, we had a pilgrimage to the Holy Land planned, with you. When the plane landed in New York on a layover, my phone

rang. My son, Joshua, who runs my business while I'm gone, said, 'Dad, we had a terrible fire in the shopping center right next door to us. There are 10-12 fire engines out there. The fire, a grease fire, completely consumed the diner—[we're right next door]—*and it burned everything down. But we're still here. I didn't realize it until I walked out the back door, the closest door to the fire. There's the fire chief and big fireman with an axe. I said, "What are you doing here?" They were getting ready to knock down the door. "We don't have a fire here," I told him. And the fire chief said, "That's impossible. Are you sure?" And my son said, 'Come in.' Nothing was wrong. The smoke went down the line of all the stores in the shopping center, but none of our walls had smoke damage. There was no fire! The fire chief was just flabbergasted. And it was a 10-foot wall, and the fire wall was only seven feet. At least three feet were unprotected from the diner next door. That diner is still not open after all these years. The fire should have scorched us unbelievably. We should have been gone. What a blessing, thanks be to God!"*

The Zsebedics love priests just as the Dupy family does. Paul Zsebedics began praying for priests in 2005, when then-associate pastor at St. Martin's Catholic Church, Fr. Dan Leary, asked him and other parishioners to pray for their shepherds. The prayer put into context a recurring dream Paul had had for 17 years:

"In the dream, I was always walking up a set of stairs. I'd see a door and always feel evil behind the door. I was consumed by the darkness, and I'd feel nothing. Just evil sort of physically beating on me, and then I'd wake up. After I first met you, Father, and was blessed by you with holy oil, I mentioned I always felt the presence of evil around me. You thought it could be some hatred toward me, and this hatred would manifest itself like a curse. Shortly after my

blessing, I started to get a pulsation of a Cross in my forehead. I couldn't figure it out, but you said it was a form of grace. You said this was removing it. I felt the evil dissipate and grace come upon me in a form of peace. I was so in tune with this pulsing that things happened soon after. I'd tell my wife, and 40 seconds later, we'd avoid a car accident. I could feel this Cross protecting me.

"After I received this peace, I had the dream again. Only this time, it was different. I was consciously praying the Our Father this time, and as I approached the door, I felt the strength of inner peace. The door opens. This is the first time I've come through. I'm in a room. I never made it this far before. I always was being attacked. Across the room are three men. I kept walking toward them, with the strength of prayer—the Our Father—saying it over and over again. I saw this man who looked like a big goon, a big tough guy. I never stopped praying. He looked at me and said: 'Listen to me.' And then he screamed, and his face morphed into something very demonic: 'STOP PRAYING FOR PRIESTS!' When I awoke, it felt like it wasn't a dream—it was real. I still had this sense of peace and I didn't have any horror of the dream.

"God has given me great grace to open my eyes to see the supernatural in the priesthood, the healing hands, the healing Masses, any healing I received in my own life—it all came from the priesthood. Can you imagine if there were no priests? God gave His single greatest gift so we can continue to receive Jesus through the priesthood, if you understand the supernatural element of Holy Hands. I've taken priests for granted all my life. I now recognize they are in persona Christi, these holy hands, ordained by Christ."

These two men's lives have been transformed through their realization of the holy priesthood. They're attuned to the supernatural in their lives. They're more grateful, more aware. They recognize when something comes between them and their faithfulness. And yet, what can come between them and their love of Christ? A fire? The Evil One? No. Nothing. No one. For they are the Salt of the Earth, the Light of the World!

Let your light shine before others, so that we may give glory to our Father in Heaven! ~ΑΩ

> *"It is with the smallest brushes that the artist paints the most exquisitely beautiful pictures."*
>
> ~ *St. André Bessette*

Afterword

At Le Grand Séminaire de Montréal, on a Friday evening, May 21, 1993, I was ordained to the deaconate. Three days later, on a trip enabled by a benefactor who knew my love of the Church and the Holy Father, I was in Pope John Paul II's personal chapel in the Vatican. The trip and the visit were gifts for my deaconate ordination. Everything had been arranged. I had a distant cousin who knew the personal secretary of the Holy Father, Stanisław Dziwisz (now Cardinal Dziwisz), to whom a request was made that I assist at a Mass with the Holy Father.

As Deacon Machado, I can say with all humility the Mass was an experience that influenced everything in my life thereafter. I was invited along with a few others, and when we arrived, we saw that the door to the private chapel was open. I'll always remember this very striking image: The Holy Father was prostrate before the altar preparing for Mass. The altar itself was simple, and prominent was the great miraculous icon and great love of the Pope's: The Black Madonna of Częstochowa, tied to the history of Poland for the past six hundred years.

Throughout the Mass, the Holy Father was present, but supernaturally he seemed to be in another world, in the mystical world of the Eucharist, in spiritual communion with the Lord. I felt Christ present with the Holy Father as I never had before. The day was May 24, 1993.

It was the first time I'd experienced the Eucharist at that level. It was very profound. The Holy Father, in hearing the word of God, the readings at the Mass, was listening attentively. He was listening with great spiritual insight to every word, every pause, shaking his head at every word, as if it were spoken by God, which it is. I never heard readings the same way after that, after seeing the Pope listening—to every breath, to every punctuation, to everything as if dictated by the Lord Himself. And all during the Mass, the Holy Father was extremely deliberative in gesture and in word. Everything was done with veneration.

An Infinite Abyss of Mercy

I was just three days removed from my ordination, and it was only the second time I'd celebrated solemnly as a deacon. But here I was in the Vatican City-State, in the papal chapel, serving the Vicar of Christ. Although I was self-conscious, his confidence made me careful and deliberative. The Holy Father looked deep into my eyes. It was as if Christ Himself was standing there before me, and I was serving Christ at the altar.

During consecration of the Holy Eucharist, it was as if time stopped. I was kneeling next to the Holy Father. It seemed like a moment that held an eternity of worship. I could feel Christ, not his vicar who was Christ, but Christ Himself who showed Himself, manifested Himself at the altar. Our Holy Father's thanksgiving after communion was in profound recollection, a recollection so profound, that it triggered in us, there at Mass, a sense to be recollected. It was as if we were immersing ourselves in the infinite abyss of Divine Mercy, an infinite ocean of Divine Mercy. It lasted 20 minutes.

At the end of Mass, after we divested in our respective sacristies, The Holy Father greeted the group, about eight in all. I mentioned I was a deacon from Montreal, and he gave me special blessing and a rosary, so that I would be consecrated to our Blessed Mother. Few experiences in my life have been as formative. To this day, I try to emulate the Holy Father's reverence for our Lord in all aspects of my ministry, especially at Holy Mass.

I wouldn't celebrate Mass again with the Pope until 1999, at the beatification of Padre Pio, concelebrating with hundreds of priests, bishops, archbishops, and cardinals. It was extraordinarily edifying for my priestly vocation.

It is through the continued example of leaders in the Roman Catholic Church, and through her holy priests, that I'm able to continue my mission to preach the Word of God. It is though the person of Jesus Christ and His Holy Sacraments that I continue to witness tremendous liberation from the effects of sin and illness—body, heart, mind, and soul. I see people entering more deeply into the mysteries and participation in the Faith after their initial evangelization and initiation. I see priests, who understand theologically what they're doing, and—on a practical level —grow in the understanding of the dignity of their ministry in Christ, and they identify more with that call.

They realize it's not because of *their* personality or any extraordinary talent or gifts or aptitudes that they're able to administer these holy gifts. *It is Christ's!* All priests have the same powers received through the grace of Holy Orders, with the bishops the moderator of their charisms. It's the potentiality and the exercise and development of those powers and through the formation of them that they become true Men of God.

As my fellow priests and I grow in this recognition of Christ working through us, I continue to see what I've been given as a seed of the Faith, in a promising way, a way that is brought to birth each day. I'm here to form, teach, heal, and expand my gifts. I'm here to act in the person of Christ, to deliver people from evil, in communion and in obedience with the Church. I'm here to rediscover with my brothers in the priesthood the role of who the priest is, because over time, the gift of the priesthood has become forgotten or obscured.

Praised be to Jesus Christ, who comes to us through hands that He chooses to make holy, and to make His own! ~ ☧

Acknowledgements

My grateful thanks to Fred and Leslie Dupy; Paul and Ellen Zsebedics; and Loretta Granger for making this book possible. I also thank all those dedicated and zealous friends and contributors who have made my ministry possible.